AFFIRMATIONS

AFFIRMATIONS

by a Group of American Anglo-Catholics, Clerical and Lay

Edited by

BERNARD IDDINGS BELL

1938

SHEED AND WARD

London and New York

PRINTED IN THE U. S. A.
BY THE HADDON CRAFTSMEN,
CAMDEN, NEW JERSEY,
FOR SHEED & WARD
63 FIFTH AVENUE,
NEW YORK

FIRST PRINTING, AUGUST, 1938

CONTENTS

FOREWORD

CHRISTIANITY in our time is subject to two dangers. One is the frontal attack of skepticism, attempting to overthrow the faith. In effect such opposition has always been salutary, a stimulus to the mind and will. The other menace, more deadly to the Church and proceeding from foes in its own household, is an uncertainty of thought which undermines the foundations of belief.

Christian apologetic, in mistaken efforts of defense, has often retreated to the weaker position, accepting literally the apologetic attitude and surrendering the sign of faith for that more doubtful symbol, the question mark. If it be true that controversialists are found usually to be wrong in denial and right in affirmation, the maxim may be taken to explain in part the temper of this book. The authors have taken positive positions which invite confidence and impart conviction. Their purpose, as described by one of them, is the adventure of battling for the Christian faith and the Christian Church. Another makes the same appeal to those who are engaged in Christian ministry, accustomed to "the idea of battling with the forces of darkness and evil for a human soul."

The writers are moved, however, by more than ardor for a holy cause. Theirs is zeal inspired by knowledge. They approach their task from many angles, prepared and proved through long experience in different fields of scholarship: in history, theology, letters, industry, art, philosophy and education. All of them have filled chairs as professors in American universities. Most of them still do. Differing in original religious background, they have thought their way to a common championship of sound Catholic faith and practice,—themselves understanding. Therefore they are able to make clear to others what and why they believe.

In the confusion which has overtaken a bewildered world, diverse courses have of late been followed by many who have grown discouraged in the quest of truth. Some, with eyes closed to the new outlook, cling obstinately to the old. Others, moved to despair by changes they cannot deny, take comfort in what shreds of conviction may be left to them. Still others, yielding to the fallacy of a false liberalism, are led to seek truth everywhere until, disillusioned, they find it nowhere.

To all such, the writers of this volume bring equal reassurance and rebuke. They picture modern life with painful accuracy, concealing nothing of its perplexity and anguish. Yet, as they present the facts in terms of human sin and divine forgiveness, of suffering and deliverance, the light in which the problem is revealed discloses also the solution. The analysis and remedy of the evils which afflict mankind are found in the content of the Catholic Creeds. These are interpreted in the book as more than intellectual assent to something.

Faith is shown to rise above the acceptance of propositions to the realm of personal trust in somebody, to "confidence in God the Father . . . implicit trust in Jesus Christ . . . unreserved commitment of oneself into the hands of God the Holy Ghost."

One closes this book with renewed conviction that genuine scientific thought, human experience and Christian belief all reach their goal as they "come in the unity of the faith and of the knowledge of the Son of God . . . unto the measure of the stature of the fullness of Christ." Apart from that revelation, the researches of science gain no satisfaction; without the affirmation of it, the Christian Church can have no unity; lacking that answer to its questions, the world will find no peace.

James DeWolf Perry

The Bishop's House
Providence, Rhode Island,
Christmas Day, 1937.

I

THE PERTINENCY OF THE CHRISTIAN FAITH

by

BERNARD IDDINGS BELL

Bernard Iddings Bell was for some years Warden of St. Stephen's College and Professor of Religion in Columbia University. He is a Bachelor of Arts of the University of Chicago, a Bachelor of Theology of the Western Theological Seminary, a Doctor of Letters of Columbia University, a Doctor of Divinity of the University of the South and a Doctor of Pedagogy of the University of the State of New York. At present he is Preaching Canon of St. John's Cathedral, Providence, Rhode Island.

THE consideration of any matter had best begin with a definition of terms. Such definition is useful in all reasoning together; but it is particularly necessary in our present venture, a discussion of the relevancy of the Christian faith; and that because almost no one nowadays seems sure of what the term Christian may mean, while there is no term more apt to be misunderstood by those who casually approach the study of religion, than is "the faith." Possibly the question of the pertinency of the Christian faith in the modern world may be at least partly on the way to solution if we understand what it is that we are talking about.

I. The Faith

"A faith" is a body of truth, or alleged truth, about God, derived from a long and co-operative using of the human reason, by generations of devotees, to arrange in order certain revelations which they are persuaded have come to them in response to the exercise of that attitude of personal entrustment which is called "faith" or "belief." A religious faith is not a body of theoretical propositions to which one is invited to give only an intellectual assent. Neither the Christian religion nor any other religion that has had prevailing power consists, or ever has consisted, of a set of opinions. Religion is not primarily something about which to debate, but, rather, a technic for personal apprehension by human beings of a God who reveals Himself.

It is significant that in the New Testament there is no word for "the faith", in the sense of a set of theological propositions; but "faith", in the sense of a personal attitude of venturesome confidence in a person (πίστις), is used nearly three hundred times. Similarly the word "belief" is found only once in the English New Testament, and there, in the Greek, the word again is πίστις. Even so it is with the verb "to believe." There are two Greek words so translated: one, νομίζω, means "to give intellectual assent" to some*thing*, while the other, πιστεύω, means "to put one's personal trust" in some*body*. The former is not translated "believe" in the English Bible; "believe" is a translation of the latter. In the vocabulary of the Christian religion, "to believe", then, *always* means "to put one's trust in" someone.

It is so, also, in a good deal other of our common speech. When a man says "I believe in my wife", he does not mean that he gives intellectual assent to the proposition that he has a wife; rather, he means that he has entire confidence in her as a wifely person. Exactly that is meant not only by the New Testament Greek word used for a religious believing, but also by the Latin word for it, *credo*. Used transitively, with the accusative, *credo* means to "commit something in trust" to somebody; intransitively, with the dative, it means "to have reliance on" somebody. Either way, it implies confidence in a person, not mere assent to a proposition. The Christian does not say, in the *Credo*, "I give consent to the fact of God the Father", or "I agree that there is an Only-Begotten Son that became incarnate", or "I concede the existence of God the Holy Ghost", or "I admit that there is One, Holy, Catholic and Apostolic Church." What he does proclaim, along with his brethren, is rather this: "I put my confidence in God the Father", and "I have implicit trust in Jesus Christ His Son the Lord", and "I give myself unreservedly into the hands of God the Holy Ghost", and "I risk my life for the sake of that mighty band of brethren, the One, Holy, Catholic and Apostolic Church."

It is worth while to devote some space to iteration of this point, because no one with a clear head on him is going to see the relevancy of the faith to anything at all so long as he regards that faith only as a set of theoretical propositions, to be perhaps conceded, instead of as a series of personal entrustments.

"The faith", then, is not primarily a matter of philosophy, but of entrustment to a God Who reveals Himself. When undergraduates come, as often they do, and say that they receive little help in the solution of religious difficulties from professors in philosophy, but rather a greater bewilderment, one may always reply, "What did you expect? A philosopher is the last man you ought to think of consulting for primary guidance in religion." One must always add, "Do not misunderstand. You can go to the philosopher, and you must go; but *last*, not first. Just as you cannot have a philosophy of science unless you first know something of science as an experience; just as you cannot have a philosophy that analyzes beauty with any competence, until first you know at least a little beauty as something to be pursued and enjoyed when found; even so you cannot have a philosophy of religion until you have begun to experience religion, or at the very least until you know that it is something in terms of which others have had experience, and do still have it." The faith, be it repeated, is not primarily a matter of philosophy. It is a formulation of what has been discovered by way of faith, by way of confidence in God and entrustment of mind and soul to Him Who reveals Himself.

If one says that man does not discover truth in any such way as that, then to that one the faith has, and can have, no relevancy whatever. To him who thinks that the only truth is "scientific truth", truth discovered by measuring concrete things and forces, religion is necessarily nonsense, since the nature of God is not discernible in terms only of matter and energy. The being of God may, indeed, be inferred from those laws of nature which have been scientifically ascertained. Most reputable scientists say that the existence of God is easier to credit, in view of the order of nature, than His non-existence. But religion, by definition (in the Oxford Dictionary, for instance), is not merely a recognition of some higher unseen power as creator and sustainer of that which is, but also an acknowledgment of that power as entitled to reverence, worship and obedience. Religion involves love to what gods there be, or dread of them, or both of these at once; it requires much more than a pleasant theorizing about the supernatural. Knowing God is far more than knowing about Him.

We do not know any persons, human or divine, by Science only. Knowing my dear friend is not a matter of weighing him or her, measuring, classifying; much more is involved, a super-scientific element, a mystic element. It is real knowledge that I get about my friend in that extra-scientific way, knowledge far more intimate and valuable than any that Science can reveal. I get to know my friend by way of response to that friend's self-revelation, a response possible only by virtue of my faith in that friend. Similarly man gets to know the Supreme Person, whose mind outbreathes and thus creatively sustains the universe, only by loving Him; and such loving, and knowing, can come only by way of faith—not by my saying "I accept the proposition that Thou art," but rather by affirming "I put my trust in Thee."

But a religious knowledge, the result of such responsive entrustments, is not a merely individual matter, any more than aesthetic knowledge is a matter only of what an individual happens to think pretty, or scientific knowledge a matter of what one single laboratory experimenter happens to be persuaded may be true. The reactions of one scientific man to the great body of objective fact, or those of one generation of scientists, are added to that which others have discovered in the past, enriching it, augmenting it, sometimes correcting it and at length sure to be corrected by it, but only a part of it; and thus *mutually* man arrives at knowledge of scientific truth. Similarly, each man's experience of beauty, or that of a single generation or epoch, is added to the great body of such experience of beauty, past and present, augmenting it, enriching it, sometimes correcting it and in the end certain to be corrected by it, but only a part of it; and thus mutually men arrive at knowledge of aesthetics. And so, as well, each man's reaction to the self-revelation of God, or that of one period of history or of those living in terms of one culture, is added to the great body of such understanding past and present, augmenting it, enriching it, sometimes correcting it and at last inevitably corrected by it, but only a part of it; and so emerges mutually man's comprehension of the necessary laws governing commerce with the Infinite. Man has experienced that-which-is in terms of objective fact, and thence comes Science; experienced that-which-is in terms of beauty, and thence arise the Arts; experienced that-which-is in terms of personality, and thence comes Religion.

Science, the Arts, Religion are all responses to an objective reality. None of them is introspective in character. Introspection is an enemy of knowledge. Introspective Science is a contradiction in terms. So is an introspective Art. So is introspective Religion. If I would know, I must forget myself and pursue the Other-than-I. That is true of all the paths to knowing; of all of them—Science, the Arts, Religion.

A sound religion, then, comes not from one's individual looking within oneself, but rather from a shared reaction to a self-revealing God, a God apart from man, though in touch with man—the technic of a confidence come at mutually. An individual creed is like an individualistic statement of scientific law or an individualistic formulation of aesthetics—of no importance to speak of. It is only a group-tested, age-tested creed which has much, if any, relevance: the formulation of what has been discovered by the response to God made by many souls. If one can but come to share in the experience which such a faith involves and reveals, he can live out his life bravely and with calmness, confident that he will learn something and get somewhere.

There must be *authority*, then, behind any valid creed; and one must submit himself or herself to that authority. Else there will be no learning of anything much about God or about man's destiny in the light of God. There are those who find such submission intolerable; but such an attitude is more than a little ridiculous, in any field of learning.

Imagine a young woman, for example, deciding to study chemistry—but scornfully, or perhaps only serenely, both disregarding the objective reality of chemical phenomena and ignoring all that former chemists have discovered in approach to that objective reality. She would come to nothing in chemistry. She might, just possibly, light for herself on one or two tiny truths; but even those she would never understand, because they would remain unrelated to other truths, of which she knew nothing but which her fathers in the Science had discovered to be true.

Chemists do not deny objective fact or despise tradition. They accept, on authority, an immense amount of dogmatic teaching. Our young chemist welcomes chemical dogma and goes to work herself, assuming that what she is dogmatically told is indeed the truth. She also learns the chemical technic, by way of long, hard practice. She may, all her life long, discover not one new thing; but at least she is happy to find that, for her as for others, certain things are indeed so. She makes those tested truths her own, and is thereby a wiser woman. It may be that she does discover some single bit of truth never before discovered, and adds it to the dogma, having persuaded others to test the validity of what she thinks is her discovery. It may be that about some small matter she proves that the chemists who have preceded her did not quite understand, shows them a significant fact or two that they have not yet perceived. But even then she is most courteous to the chemical tradition, knowing that, in vastly the greater part, it is much more right than she or any other single experimenter.

Or imagine a young man who decides to be a painter but has no patience with tradition and no realization of the objectivity of Beauty. He will not learn the laws of perspective or of chiaroscuro, or any laws at all; but, like a savage, he will splash his paint crudely about and see what he gets. Sometimes such a fellow sells his paintings, and even acquires reputation, for a day, among the ignorant or with poseurs; but he is no painter. The artist must go to school, and patiently learn the dogma of his art. Having learned it, it may be that, under some great inspiration, he can transcend that dogma and create some work of genius greater than the dogma alone could inspire; but even then he never ceases to have respect for the fundamentals of his art.

Even so it is in religion; but not all people, especially in these rather silly days, seem to understand it. Tell the average person that the first step in religion is to submit to authority, and that that governs also the second step, and the third, and so on, probably for years, before ever one can walk alone, and he or she promptly gets offended. Urged on, perhaps, by some elderly flatterer who burbles pleasantly of freedom and self-expression, (without bothering to define freedom or to understand what self may be), young persons are all too apt to start talking about obscurantism and similar bogies, and to demand a license in respect to religion that they never think of asking in laboratory or studio. They demand to be completely informed and convinced about God before beginning, or continuing, the practice of religion. How is such conviction possible, without regard for the objectivity of God or respect for the discoveries of the past and submission to the religious technic prescribed by the experience of the race? Casual speculation will no more alone reveal the being and nature of God, or the possible relationship of God to man, than it will reveal the Mendelian law or the secret of the Brahms Requiem. What they really want, these strangely unreasonable young rationalists, is to have God "throw a miracle" to convince them. God will not do it. Knowledge is not imparted by way of cataclysmic fiat. There is no bowling over of lazy people into wisdom.

The Faith, then, is the formulation of what has been discovered when man has made venture of trust in a creative and self-revealing Personal Being who exists beneath, behind, beyond the sensible universe.

The Faith is expressed, of necessity, in symbolic language. All personal relationships are so expressed. But it is, for all that, a symbolic formulation of reaction to reality, tested by the ages, tested still today. As such, the Faith has relevancy, pertinency, applicability nowadays, in exactly the same way that the laws discovered by scientists and the dogmatic canons governing artists have relevancy, pertinency, applicability. None of these comprises all the truth that man will ever discover; but they are the best he knows now, after ages of response to revelation; and that is quite enough to justify respect from them that have desire to learn. Most rejecters of tradition, in any field, are intellectual dilettantes, more lazy than brave, less creative innovators than blowers-off of steam. In every field of life it is the traditionalists who lead in progress, the dogmatists who dare.

II. *The Christian Faith*

But are there not many formulations of faith, all entitled to respect and for precisely the reason given above? To what degree, if at all, has the Christian

Faith an especial claim to adequacy and relevancy? Why may we not just as well go forth to live according to the Buddhist Faith or that of Mahomet or that of the followers of Zoroaster?

The first thing to do with that question is for the questioner to examine himself, to make sure that in asking it he is entirely honest. Is he really determined to follow *some* formulation of religious experience, and only in doubt about *which one* to adopt; or is he seeking an excuse for inaction, saying that since all must be good, he will go the way of none but, rather, will stop stock-still and vegetative, in the spot where he now happens to be? Is this person who doubts the finality of the Christian Faith seriously out to arrive at completion of knowledge; or is he, perhaps, like a grievously sick man who might say, "There are many physicians whom I might summon for the diagnosis and cure of my disease, all of them good, possibly equally good; but I am not sure which of these doctors is absolutely the best, and I shall summon none at all", and so dies? There are indeed other faiths beside the Christian one, some of them wise and perceptive and helpful; and certainly any of the tried and tested faiths is better than no faith; but any of them must be accepted, believed and followed before it can help to real knowing. To hesitate too long, unwilling to choose between them, is apt to be not merely useless but cowardly.

Still, the question is often both bravely and honestly asked. The inquirer really would like to know why the Christian Faith is a better faith than the others.

To answer such a man by a simple and sweeping assertion that it is, and there must be no argument about it, is poor apologetics. One must convince the inquirer, who does not believe, of at least a probable superiority, before he will sufficiently invest himself to discover the absolute superiority. This is not the place for a scientific disquisition on comparative religion, the study of which clearly shows to most dispassionate students many probabilities about the relative truth of Christianity when compared with other faiths. All that this paper can do, in addition to having suggested the pertinency of having some sort of religious faith, is to point out at least one way, and that not too commonly noted, in which the Faith that has grown up by way of reaction to God's revelation of Himself in Jesus Christ, has more probable relevancy today than the other faiths possess. What follows is no final argument for Christianity, but only one consideration toward a persuasion of the man who admits the general relevancy of religion but hesitates about *what* religion should be his.

That minor but significant argument runs this way: Why go to a civilization alien to one's own for one's religion, any more than for one's arts? It is a difficult thing to do. To most of us, traditional Chinese music is a mystery of jangling dissonance, alien to the ear, while both Japanese painting and Balinese ceremonial dancing seem strangely exotic. Similarly, in religion, when I read the *Avesta* of Zarathustra, I find Mazda interesting but very odd. I can look into the *Upanishads*; but *Vedanta* remains to me an alien way of thinking about life, and involves an alien way of living it. Indian mythology is, to an Occidental, weirdly nightmare-like, and Indian ceremonial even inducive of a certain nausea. The maxims of Confucius or Lao Tzu are probably forever incomprehensible, at least as an adequate answer to the mysteries of life, to any except those who have lived under Chinese familism. Oriental religions are alien to Occidental civilization. Why pursue them in preference to a way indigenous in our own culture?

Moreover, the cultures that produced these other religions seem to be disappearing, or at best declining. One occasionally still hears someone ascribe to Oriental civilizations a toughness, an age-old vigor, that insures their eventual continuance when Occidental civilization has perished. To say that, is almost incredibly to disregard the facts of modern world development. Oriental *races* may well survive and flourish when Western races are no more, especially if the latter continue in the racial suicide which results from birth-control; but the Oriental *civilizations* are decadent. Japan is a Western nation in respect to industry, commerce, politics, armament, even costume and cosmetics. It is like the West, only rather more so. Chinese civilization will go the same way; and indeed most Chinese thinkers seem definitely to wish it to do so as quickly as possible. And all the poetic heroisms of Gandhi cannot slow down the transformation of Indian civilization by the impacts of Western science and the steam machine. Dr. Wei, one of the leading educators in China, has said, "The

Orient is desperate to get the power and skill which Western science and Western political organization can bring. Modern schools . . . the whole educational system completely revolutionized . . . returned students from the West in the important position in politics, industry, learning, commerce." Social disintegration of what was the East seems inevitable; reintegration into a new West equally inevitable. Japan is not dangerous to Europe and America nor is a possibly nationalized India, because they are continuing unchanged their Oriental, alien civilizations, very ancient and odd; but precisely because they now begin to have Occidental civilizations, very new. Their people are exceedingly able and eager, impatiently restless to fulfill a new-accepted destiny. We have a fear that they may be indeed even as we, only more competent.

The more dynamic elements in these countries, those elements that are more and more in control of the new East, have found, and more and more find, that the religions of the old East, their old spiritual technics, are incompatible with the Occidental *geist* that increasingly prevails. It is a great deal easier for a modern Oriental to accept an Occidental religion than for a modern Occidental to find help in any of the religions of the Orient.

Providentially Christianity, which originated at the time and place where East and West divided and went their several ways, turned for its life and growth toward the dynamic West instead of toward the static East, the rational West instead of the introspective

East. Thus it happens that, as the static and mystical East becomes at last, in this our day, also dynamic and rational, Christianity becomes as relevant to life and thought in one part of the planet as in another. It, and it alone among religions, has pertinency for the world that is coming to be.

This has its chief bearing, perhaps, in discussion of the rationale of Missions; but here one may note it merely to justify advising him who would seek God to accept the Christian Faith, the Christian formulation of human reaction to God's revelation of Himself in Jesus (rather than to commit himself to any other of the great religions), with surety that Christianity is probably more valuable to him than any faith that has prevailed in terms of living, feeling, thinking, that are past or passing. Assurance of the complete and absolute truth of Christianity must, for such a person, wait on *venture* of faith.

Christianity is at one with the attitude toward life which is coming into increased maturity, rather than with that of a day which is dying. It may be that a good part, even the greater part, of our world will abandon all Religion, at least for awhile; but if so, when it recovers, as it inevitably must recover, its hunger for Reality in personal terms—for God, the hunger which leads men to Religion, it will do so in terms of a post-modern life and thought with which the Oriental faiths are incompatible. It may well be that the religion of the future will be more perfectly Christian than any yet seen; but it will certainly not be a religion neo-Parsee, nor neo-Vedantist, nor neo-

Confucianist, nor neo-Mohammedan. The only religious tradition, the only faith, which has world relevancy today, is Christianity,–the religion that, under God, has grown along with that dynamic, rational way of life which more and more takes possession of the earth.

II

CHRISTIANITY OR CHAOS

by

WILLIAM AYLOTT ORTON

William Aylott Orton came from the Industrial Relations Department of the British Ministry of Labor, in 1922, since when he has been Professor of Economics in Smith College. From time to time he has lectured also in Bryn Mawr, Amherst and the University of California. He is a Master of Arts of Cambridge University and a Master of Science of the University of London.

THE PAST two decades have been extraordinarily prolific of philosophies of history. Spengler, Pareto, Friedell, Croce, Bukharin, Sorokin, Toynbee, Whitehead, Wells, Russell, Mumford, Ortega, Berdyaev and many others, including both physicists and psychoanalysts, have been drawn into the enterprise; while words have become deeds in the contest between the mechanistic dogma of the Russians, the biological dogma of the Germans, and the aggressive atavism of Italy.

The vogue is not surprising. In the forty years of material expansion that followed the Franco-Prussian war, it was possible for the not-too-curious to find sufficient meaning for the human adventure in the "progress" of mundane events. Not yet was it apparent that that expanding universe was going to burst. Rationalism, agnosticism, positivism, could all unite in optimistic chorus under the baton, say, of Frederick Harrison, the English exponent of Comte:

> "We all know those noble choruses of Handel, and have heard the opening notes begin simple, subdued, and slow, until they are echoed back in deeper tones, choir answering to choir, voice joining in with voice, growing fuller and stronger with new and varying bursts of melody, until the whole stream of song swells into one vast tide of harmony, and rolls on abounding, wave upon wave of majestic exultation and power. Something

> like this complex harmony is seen in the gathering parts of human history, age taking up the falling notes from age, race joining with race in answering strain, until the separate parts are mingled in one, and pour on in one movement together."[1]

But the final movement of the symphony was not yet written; and when at last history set the score before them, the singers, appalled at its hideous cacophony, flung up their parts and went home—to find, in the metaphorical and often in the literal sense, that there was no longer any home to go to.

After the crash—or was it merely the first warning? —the dogma of progress faded before a more imminent chaos. The search for a meaning in history became a desperate matter, in which a greater number of people engaged. The prospect of sheer chaos, or inanity, is definitely unacceptable to the mind; and the more obvious such a prospect becomes, the more eagerly do men look for some fiction to disguise it. Even a tragic plot is more bearable than no plot at all. Accordingly, the two heroes of the saga of progress now reappear as the two villains of the saga of violence.

That optimistic theory of human nature which the seventeenth century had devised to suit its anti-authoritarian mood, and which succeeding centuries had adopted under a variety of high-sounding names—social instinct, benevolent sympathy, spontaneous sociability, and so forth—became suddenly the "herd instinct" of Trotter and his school. Men who had

[1] *The Meaning of History* (1894), Ch. 1.

conceived of themselves as only a little lower than the angels (in whom they did not believe) now discovered that they were only a little higher than the brutes (whose existence they could not deny). Not a few, therefore, essayed to handle human society as a herd is handled. This was the inevitable outcome of shouting that all men were brothers, while denying that they had a common Father. And today, psychologists who are certain that there is nothing to be learned from theology, appropriately direct their studies to the behavior of anthropoids; no doubt, with significant results.

Similarly, the faith in applied science that wafted a previous generation so comfortably toward a real and peaceful Utopia leaves the present generation stranded on a shore which is neither real (Platonic paradox!) nor peaceful. Says Friedell, alluding to the scientific marvels of cinema and radio:

> "The human voice has achieved omnipresence, the human gesture eternity, but at the cost of the soul. It is the Tower of Babel: 'And the Lord said: Go to, let us go down, and there confound their language, that they may not understand one another's speech.' We already have nightingale concerts and Papal speeches alike transmitted by wireless. Here indeed is the 'Decline of the West.' There are no realities any more, there is only apparatus. It is a world of automata, conceived in the brain of a malicious and crazy Doctor Miracle."[2]

But the devil was always something of a humorist. Having intoxicated science with the method of meas-

[2] *Cultural History of the Modern Age*, Vol. III, p. 475.

urement until it was prepared to deny existence to whatever could not be measured, he now sees with a chuckle the method pushed to its utmost refinement, at which point matter itself politely declines to exist any longer. Meanwhile the adolescent "science" of sociology, more naive even than the science of physics, becomes in turn bemused with the method of measurement; and society, visibly dying from within, derives what comfort it can from an elegant shroud of statistics.

A peaceful end, however, is more than applied science can promise. Instead, it implements the prophecy of war—to which in such abundance it furnishes the means. Let Professor Laski, for the modern age, reply to Frederick Harrison:

> "The essential purpose of the state is always to protect a given system of class relations. . . . So far, on the evidence of history, any class which has sought to redefine its position in the state, in any fundamental way, has always had to achieve its ends by violent revolution. . . . To make such a change in terms of peace involves, in a period of crisis, the conquest of the emotions by reason. There is no experience more rare in the history of the human race. It is unlikely to be our experience where what is affected by the change is the basic factor in all social relationships. The peaceful evolution of institutions depends for its realization upon the ability of men to agree upon the purposes they must have in view; their solidarity is a function of that agreement. And the agreement must be more than a merely verbal one; it must be daily realized in the lives of average men and women. The signs are about us on every hand that this agreement is no longer possible."[3]

[3] *The State* (1935), pp. 294-8.

II

That agreement never was possible: not at any time when the "interests they must have in view" were conceived, in Laski's terms, as those of separate economic classes competing for larger shares of a limited gross income. Woodrow Wilson put the matter quite succinctly when he said, in reply to a lot of loose talk about common interests, "Interest does not unite men; interest separates men; the only thing that unites men is a common devotion to right."

From the perennial class-wars of the Greek city-states to the generalized class-war of today, history attests the soundness of Laski's deduction from Laski's premises. But when he goes on to suggest that a solution can be found in the abolition of all classes, and an identity "daily realized in the lives of average men and women" of economic purposes, the muse deserts him. This supposed homogeneity of a supposed classless society is a myth of the intellectuals. There never was such a society—not even on the scale of the city-states—and history suggests that there never will be. The proletarian revolution results, not in a dictatorship of the proletariat, but in a dictatorship over the proletariat. Conflicting group interests emerge, and are resolved by authority and force, alike under Fascism, Nazism and Communism. The work of the class executioner is never finished, and only the music of a strident nationalism conceals it. You sing or you suffer.

Not that the ideal of eliminating class conflict is to

be decried. On the contrary, in Christian tradition a social system which produces perennial class conflict is *ipso facto* condemned, no matter what else it may produce, nor in what abundance. What is wrong is the assumption that the innumerable class conflicts of modern society can be got rid of by summing them all up in one grand, ultra-simplified class war. That idea is irretrievably academic. It has never ceased to smell of the British Museum. Out in the streets society, like nature, like life, is manifold, rich, complex, flashing with conflict not only of good and evil, but of good and better, adumbrating a harmony, a peace, which is never realized in the here and now and which seems indeed the more remote as one ascends from inanimate, through animate, to sentient existence. The path to its meaning, as many are now discovering, does not lie along the road of abstraction. Something indeed must be "daily realized in the lives of average men and women," but no mere theory will suffice.

The attempt to eliminate class conflict by a single drastic generalization was made once before, by the theorists of the French revolution. The monarchy in France had become associated with, and at last controlled by, an economic oligarchy—not through any inherent necessity, but through the weakness and corruption of sinful men who had been amply warned. The revenge of the masses swept both away. Then came the grand over-simplification. Since the capitalist corporations had been oppressive, there were to be no more groups or associations of any sort whatever. As Hegel said, "fanaticism wills an abstraction." The famous law of le Chapelier (of course, he was a lawyer) made it a crime, not only for people to associate on the basis of their "pretended common interests", but for anyone even to encourage the spirit of association. Henceforth there were to be only the State on top and the disintegrated mass of individuals below: an atomic theory of society embodying all the fallacies of the atomic theory of physics.

That dagger of dialectic, stuck into the heart of Europe, prepared the way for the tyranny of the modern State and the eventual battle of the tyrants. The older and more humane forms of association never recovered from the blow: not only in France, but wherever French ideology, along with French idealism, had taken root. It took roughly seventy years to remove the taint of criminality from ordinary working men's unions. Abstract capital alone received its freedom—nay, its arrogant license—to combine in pursuit of abstract wealth. The tradition of true corporate life disappeared. Meanwhile, the claim to exclusive sovereignty of the secular State led to a widening revolt against sovereignty itself; nihilism, anarchism, communism, syndicalism, became popular; while the State, unable by its nature to rise above economic group interest, inevitably led the masses into mutual slaughter. No wonder that Bertrand Russell, looking at the record, declared: "every increase in the strength of the State has been a new disaster to mankind."

By any measure, war is now civilization's major enterprise. Even in America, its annual cost exceeds the gross income of the largest industry. Longing for peace, men find themselves mysteriously impelled to organize for conflict. The promise of the Incarnation, "peace on earth to men of goodwill," is frustrated in a universal heartbreak. Having lost the vision of the Good—and therefore, the faith which that vision engenders—the will becomes diseased and wanders blindly in the outer darkness. Because it is no longer good, it cannot find the road to peace. Will and wish no longer move together. Without faith—and therefore without hope—men traverse a world full of heavenly beauty and earthly promise, which they cannot apprehend because they are crushed beneath an incubus of nightmare fear and ineluctable despair.

III

Looked at from another angle—that of ordinary morality—the modern impasse is no less striking. One of the major paradoxes of our time is the contrast between individual and collective standards of behavior. By and large, the majority of individuals are now decent and kindly folk. To that extent—and it is a great extent—civilization has succeeded.

When we regard these same individuals in their collective capacities, the picture changes. There is less of which to be proud. These same people, who as individuals show so much natural goodness, cheat and lie and steal and kill on the grand scale, once they become "organized." As voters in local and national government, as members of political machines, as stockholders in corporations, as trade unionists, brokers, advertisers, radio announcers, ordinary "business men"—people find themselves unable, in collective or public capacities, to exercise the standards of positive virtue which in their private lives they demand from themselves and from one another. "The good that I would, I do not; but the evil which I would not, that I do"—St. Paul voices the typical dilemma of the modern voter, the modern stockholder. Call an activity "business" or "politics" and you throw around it a screen of immunity to all those gentle and kindly impulses that make the world a safe place to live in.

Individuals are civilized, collectivities are not. We live under a schizoid morality; and we are so used to it that the very idea of demanding positive virtue in our dominant types of collective activity seems absurd and quixotic. But let us ask ourselves where we shall be if we fail to get it—for those group activities are what make our mortal destiny. Nay, let us look at where we are. We find the secular State, in the interests of a minimum humanity, impelled to the almost impossible task of regulating industry and business from without, because the community cannot trust those activities to regulate themselves from within; and a sort of trench warfare develops between the community as sovereign and its own constituent organizations. In truth, it is futile for a non-Christian society to rail at bureaucracy. Bureaucracy is its sole substitute for virtue.

Yet again, on the plane of ideals, the modern impasse is pathetically obvious. The exponents of the gospel of individualism saw themselves as the heralds of the age of freedom. By the destruction or secularization (it is the same thing) of corporate life, they released a flood of economic energy which was supposed to float the masses towards at least a material Utopia. A considerable advance was indeed made. But more. Their positive ideals, taken over from Christianity, were, as far as they went, valid and noble. Personal freedom and international peace, let us remember, were intrinsic parts of *laissez faire* philosophy. In this direction, also, much was accomplished. None the less, the age of liberalism has been the age of war; its climax, the greatest war in history; its sequel, a widespread disdain of personal liberty; its legacy, chaos and confusion. Why?

The answer is: because the material and the spiritual ideals of individualism were fundamentally incompatible. The free operation of the profit motive was not compatible with the ideal of general personal freedom. The operation of the principle of free international trade was not compatible with the ideal of lasting international peace. These are not matters of theory, but matters of fact. And since, to an adequate concept of reason, history is not irrational, the causes thereof can be discerned. Their description is one of the major tasks of the Church today.

IV

Personal freedom and social peace are not contrasting, or even separable, ideals; they are fundamentally associated. In the last analysis, both are reflections of the ultimate reality of human nature. Man is not born free, as Rousseau foolishly asserted. He is born with the possibility of freedom. This possibility is realized strictly in the extent to which his life is governed by its highest faculties; the idea is familiar to the most elementary student of Plato. Freedom is in fact a matter of degree, and the degrees are marked on a scale of moral and spiritual achievement. Only in this sense is personal freedom a valid ideal, or even a safe political objective; in this sense its claim is absolute.

But a man does not rise alone or unaided. He attains his full spiritual stature in Society—as Aristotle clearly pointed out.

> "A State exists for the sake of a good life, and not for the sake of life only. A State is not a mere society having a common place, established for the prevention of crime and for the sake of exchange. These are conditions without which a State cannot exist; but all of them together do not constitute a State, which is a community of well-being in families and aggregations of families, for the sake of a perfect and self-sufficing life, by which we mean a happy and honorable life. Our conclusion, then, is, that political society exists for the sake of noble actions, and not of mere companionship."[4]

The *raison d'être* of political society, in short, is spiritual achievement. Nothing less will render society either philosophically intelligible or practically workable.

These seeds of social wisdom, sown in blood and tears as the light faded over Hellas, bore their undying

[4] *Politics* (Jowett), Bk. I.

harvest in the dawn of Christendom. Transfigured and made dynamic by the Church, they contain not merely an irrefragable core of political truth, but the *only* solution time has ever offered to the problem of the individual and the community. In the language of the Church this teaching is familiar to every educated person today. It is indeed interesting to observe how, in quarters independent of the Christian tradition, leaders of education are being drawn back to it by its inner consistency and historical truth.

Translated into secular terms, this tradition insists upon a hierarchy of values, and demands that such an hierarchy be made explicit both in the pattern of the individual life and in the institutions and procedures of the social life. It asserts that unless this hierarchy be sustained, neither freedom nor peace is, as a matter of fact, possible. It teaches, with an overwhelming body of evidence, that where economic or acquisitive drives are given their head to a degree in which moral and spiritual values become secondary, Society is headed for disaster—not in some remote future or in some other world, but in the historical present of actual mundane existence.

It teaches, moreover, that no two-dimensional Utopia will fit a three-dimensional world: no scheme that promises merely more of this world's goods to more people can ensure peace, for the simple reason that appetites can always outrun the satisfactions available, and struggle must ensue. On the other hand, it teaches that when men do associate for the attainment of the spiritual values (using the term in its very widest connotation)—"wherever two or three are gathered together *in My name*"—goodwill, grace, power, light, blessing, whatever you choose to call it, does, as a matter of fact, enter into their lives; because they are "made that way".

V

Truth so fundamental as this is in the paradoxical position of being generally accepted and generally ignored. Were it merely one among a number of equally plausible hypotheses, its role would be easier of fulfilment. But the Christian tradition, as an ethical system, is confronted by no alternatives. It is the only tradition of our culture. It has had its lunatic fringe, from Mani to Machiavelli and beyond. But no other ethical system has won the adherence of any civilized Society. Even in Russia, the fundamentals of the Christian system of ethics are at least professed.

And there lies the problem. A mere assent to an ethical doctrine is practically meaningless—as the Greeks discovered. Truth that is true always makes demands upon conduct; and this, the sovereign truth about human nature, makes sovereign demands. It is therefore necessary that it be constantly held before men in the form of a challenge. That indeed is what it really is.

The Christian Church, as a social institution, exists to elicit from mankind a daily corporate affirmation of the truth of which she is the custodian: to do this, not in the form of a merely intellectual assent to ethical principles which cannot in any case be disputed, but in the form of a spiritual act of will directed towards the reality upon which those principles rest—the reality which, from Socrates onward, men have agreed to call "divine." Thus while the Church must often speak the language of the schools, of which she is the master, she alone speaks also the more immediate language of reality: which language is art and liturgy and sacrament.

In this dual endowment, this double mission, lies the essential character of the Catholic religion. This is much misunderstood. Many outside the gates, and some within, have talked as if the Church were supposed to be the sole and exclusive source of all practical and philosophical wisdom. She has never claimed that position for herself. On the contrary, none knew better than the Apostles and the early Fathers that the teaching and the practice of the Church embody a vast syncretism—which did not come to a sudden end in the fourth century. The Church accepts this, and glories in the fact. It is no news to her—though apparently it is to her opponents—that a living religion grows out of human soil, with roots that are very old and wide and deep. But the soil does not burgeon and blossom of itself, nor the fruit appear without due season.

We must believe that God chose the time and place of His revelation deliberately; or—if we prefer language that is more abstruse, though not necessarily more illuminating—that the intellectual, moral and spiritual life of mankind had reached, through endless centuries, a point at which new contact with reality suddenly became possible, charging with new significance the human past, with new promise and power the future. Those many persons to whom the 'historicity' of the Christian revelation is a major stumbling-block, owe their difficulty to a failure to think historically: as if the major event of history could have occurred at no particular time and place, for no particular reason!

VI

This weakness of the historical sense, of the human time-scale as felt in everyday life, imposes certain handicaps on the position of the Church in America, at which it is worth while to glance in conclusion.

First: the rapid spread of applied science and of pseudo-science has so affected both the material and the mental environments that it is difficult for people to realize the possibility of truth which is permanent. The difficulty appears in aesthetic as well as in mental and moral valuations. The callow culture of a mechanical age suggests, against all reason, that what was true, good, or beautiful twenty years ago, or two thousand years ago, cannot possibly be so today. Confusion and triviality naturally result. It is primarily the business of education to overcome this attitude. It cannot be said that the task is being successfully performed.

Second: with so short an experience of tradition, people who can admit the possibility of truth which is permanent tend to look for it in a formula, like the Bill of Rights or the American Constitution. The American system, as commonly conceived, has roots no deeper than eighteenth-century rationalism. To forget that is a profound and obvious error. But so sedulously have Americans been taught to believe that all their felicities spring from a particular political doctrine, recently written down on a particular piece of paper (or was it sheepskin?), that it is hard for them to get beyond the letter that killeth to the spirit which giveth life. America is the land of formulae and fundamentalism, of programs and patent medicines; and religion tends either to slip backwards to the stage of the medicine man or sideways to the stage of the popular panacea. That the business of the Church is not to make programs but to make men, seems therefore quite surprising.

Third: in the period since the Civil War, American life has become largely a technic for the deliberate evasion of spiritual experience. Alike in the sensationalism of what passes for art and literature, in the disintegration of social philosophies, and in the shallowness of its understanding of Europe, this evasion is manifest. One can point to scores of well-known Americans whose talent takes the form of an eccentric and half-conscious flight from the profundities of the inner life to the distractions of a civilization that is rapidly becoming meaningless.

Fourth: not only in America, but wherever the Christian tradition is professed without being practised, intellectual confusion has been a necessary consequence. In no respect is this confusion more patent than in the current refusal to face the doctrine of sin. It is a simple fact that when we refuse to fulfil the demands of our common patrimony a sense of failure, or of guilt, besets us. We feel and know that we have sinned and come short of the glory of God, revealed for our guidance through this difficult world. Since this feeling is uncomfortable, an age that has made a god of comfort will not admit it. In the popular lingo of pseudo-psychology and pseudo-religion, the word *sin* is banished from polite intercourse. Instead, we invent all sorts of elaborate disguises for the fact to which it refers. A deterministic dogma, for instance, comes in very handy when times are bad. Believe in it, and will (however paradoxically) to act on your belief, and the future is yours; but as to how you got into the mess, that is entirely the fault of "circumstances".

American sociology, with its trend towards uplift and reform, fulfils a similar function for a wider group. The pioneer tradition lingers in our sentimental fondness for the doctrine of free-will; but not for all its consequences. Sociology comes forward with a variety of comfortable explanations of the fact that things go wrong. You can blame, according to the school of your choice, either the "environment" (ignoring the circular argument involved); or the "culture"—that vague *ding-an-sich* suspended in a logical vacuum; or your genes, hormones and chromosomes; or that poor old scapegoat, the subconscious. You can blame, in short, almost anything except yourself. The popularity of psychoanalysis springs from a similar motivation;

and the truth which it embodies is now being rescued with difficulty from a widespread misuse.

In all these subterfuges the root-impulse is to escape the more exacting and uncomfortable phases of human responsibility, individual and collective. Catholics, as individuals, know how hard (and how salutary) it is to utter a sincere *mea culpa*. The organized masses of mankind have always found it easier to strike their enemies, real or fancied, than to strike their breasts. So difficult is it, in the prevailing flabbiness, to get people to face the consequences of their own wrong-doing that the Church is now in danger of giving up the attempt, of trimming its sails to the storm of popular passion and surrendering its pretension to universal allegiance.

VII

To turn from such considerations as these to the pages of the daily paper is like turning from one world to another. The final issue arises: which of the two is shadow, and which substance. But the contrast is not all light and darkness. There is confusion in both worlds, not alone because the secular has invaded the spiritual, but because the spiritual has so largely pervaded the secular. Precisely because the Church has not wholly failed, her role is difficult. Precisely because civilized thought is now so widely, if not deeply, Christian, the way seems more confused.

One clue is clear. Ideally, the Church is nothing less than mankind organized in its spiritual aspect. Practically, she claims the allegiance of all who accept as basic the possibility of spiritual regeneration, and combats those who do not. This distinction is sharp. To those who accept, she offers freedom with responsibility, peace with a discipline, faith with a struggle, hope with a task that is never ended. To those who deny, she offers, in intellectual, historical and practical terms, an uncompromising challenge to find a meaning in life that death cannot laugh away.

III

THE CHURCH AND MODERN THOUGHT

by

Wilbur Marshall Urban

Wilbur Marshall Urban became Professor of Philosophy in Yale in 1931, after having taught in succession at Princeton, Ursinus, Trinity and Dartmouth. He is head of the philosophy department at Yale and director of graduate studies. He is a Bachelor of Arts of Princeton, a Doctor of Letters of Trinity College and a Doctor of Philosophy of Leipzig.

WE HAVE insensibly entered upon a stage of modern thought—roughly speaking since the war—which as yet no one understands and the outcome of which no one can predict. It is full of uncertainty and paradox. It is doubtful whether there has ever been an age in which man has understood himself so little; in which he has been so knowing and yet so unaware, so burdened with purposes and yet at bottom so purposeless, so disillusioned and yet feeling himself so completely the victim of illusion. This indecision permeates our entire culture—our science and our philosophy, our industry and our art. It is not strange that it should have entered into our religion and our religious life.

Does someone doubt that these are the characters of our age? What then shall we say of an epoch in which men's industry grows ever fiercer and fiercer, while doubt of the good of the economic system under which they are working—even of its ability to survive—becomes ever more and more insistent? Of an epoch in which knowledge grows from more to more, while faith in the ultimate meaning of that knowledge becomes weaker and weaker? What shall we say of an epoch in which the means of artistic expression become ever more complicated and refined, only to leave us haunted by the feeling that there is less and less of significance to express? What, finally, shall we say of an age in which men seem to feel ever more deeply that some religion, some saving faith is necessary to the very continuance of the life of industry, of society and culture, and yet the desire and power to lay hold upon such a faith becomes ever weaker and weaker?

The entire religious life of the present is puzzling enough. But, if I mistake not, there is one point at which it appears especially paradoxical–namely the point at which religion comes into relation with science and philosophy. It has long been a commonplace that modern science has undermined men's faith. On the other hand, we are also told that not for decades, perhaps not for centuries, have science and philosophy been so favorable to religion. The puzzling thing about the situation is that, in a sense, both of these things are true. Let me first try to indicate what I think to be the meaning of this paradox and, secondly, its significance for the Church in its relation to the modern soul.

I think we may take it for granted that a significant change has come over the spirit of modern science. We have been told on all sides that modern physics has given the death blow to mechanistic and materialistic views of the world; that "no first rate biologist is a mechanist," that the overwhelming tendency is against reducing life and mind to matter. We have been told by physicist after physicist that reality is coming to appear more and more as intelligence and mind. Above all we are told that scientists are becoming philosophical, are more and more recognizing the limitations of science, and acknowledge a world of realities and values that transcend and escape their symbols.

We are told all these things, and they are in the main true. Why then, we may well ask, is this change seemingly of so little effect? If these things had happened in the Victorian era, the effect would have been electrical. They would have been seen and felt to be the very opposite of the views of science to which irreligious men had pinned their faith. If not actually demonstrating the reality of God, they at least make much more intelligible and possible the religious man's view of the world. Why do they not do that now? Why do these great changes in the intellectual outlook to such an unexpected degree leave men cold?

This is, I believe, a most important question for us men of religion, and for you who have the difficult task of the cure of modern souls. Let me suggest to you, first of all, my interpretation of the present situation.

II

That the modern man is still in the main apathetic to these stirring changes in the life of the spirit, there seems to be little doubt. Everywhere, in all the departments of man's spiritual life, there is this lack of saving faith—a wide reaching and deeply-going arrest of all his spiritual initiatives—that strange combination of illusion and disillusionment which we have come to recognize as the basal character of the modern mind.

Mr. Walter Lippmann complains that we moralists and religionists have failed to understand our times. We think that we are dealing with a generation that refuses to believe in ancient authority. We are in fact dealing with a generation that cannot believe in it. We think that we are confronted with men who have an irrational preference for immorality, whereas the men and women about us are ridden with doubts because they do not know what they prefer and why.[1]

Now I doubt very much whether we moralists and religionists are quite as ununderstanding of our times as Mr. Lippmann supposes. For myself, I can only say that it is chiefly among men of religion—among the physicians of the soul, that I find any real understanding of this spiritual paralysis which is so widespread in the modern world. Be that as it may, it will not be amiss to recall the situation to our minds once again.

The man of today, then, does not believe for the reason that, for the time being at least, he cannot. The youth of the day, for instance, is in this very curious mood. It has been given excellent expression in a Yale undergraduate publication, in an article entitled: "Religion Leaves the Colleges." The writer paints with skill and understanding a state of mind which I know only too well—a strange remoteness of the youth of today from the deeper life of men as envisaged in religion. It voices their youthful impatience with—even their contempt for—the emasculated faith which modern protestantism and liberalism seem to offer them. But it strikes an even deeper note, one which many observers of the situation do not seem to understand. A note of powerlessness—an underlying sense of disillusionment and futility, a radical incapacity to be-

[1] *A Preface to Morals*, p. 316.

lieve in anything, even in life itself. They, too, cannot believe and they know it.

I should like to dwell for a little on this student mind, but I must move on. I can only say again that the intellectual youth of today is in a very curious mood—one which we of older years find it very difficult to understand. We are likely to think that youth is naturally a period of idealism and optimism, and to think that what I have said cannot be true. None the less, for the time being at least, "the native hue of resolution is sicklied o'er with the pale cast of thought." Something has arrested youth's deepest spiritual initiatives, even those faiths which are merely social and political,—and with these the capacity for any kind of fundamental faith.

III

Of this momentary incapacity for any faith there seems, then, to be little doubt. Regarding the causes of this paralysis there seems to be an almost equal unanimity of opinion. They have been summed up in one phrase—the "acids of modernity." Those acids, we are told, have slowly but surely eaten into man's faith. They have at the same time eaten into his belief in himself and his faith in God. They have eaten God out of the universe and ideals out of his own life. They have eaten into the very capacity for faith itself.

The acids of modernity! What an arresting, what a significant phrase! The really significant question, however, is what these acids are. Like most students of the present situation, I hold that these acids have, in a sense, and to a degree, been secreted by modern science. But this is only part of the truth. Modern science is only the secondary, not the primary, cause of our situation. Our loss of faith is primarily moral, and only secondarily intellectual. The acids of modernity have been chiefly secreted by modern life itself.

Something in modern life has been poisoning the very springs of life itself. What this something is has been vaguely described as the materialization and mechanism of life, and these terms will do as well as any. It has been said that the modern man's daily experiences with life, as it is now lived, somehow make instinctively incredible those unconscious ideas that are at the core of the religious life. My thesis is that those ideas have become incredible because the moral and spiritual values that underlie them are no longer real. With loss of faith in life has gone the loss of faith in all those things which have hitherto given life its meaning. If God's in his Heaven, then all's right with the world. But if something is very wrong with life and with the world—if life, and the world in which our life is lived, is felt to be basically meaningless and unintelligible—men cannot then, you may be sure, find God in the Heavens.

Only thus, I think, can we understand this progressive paralysis of faith that has crept over the modern man. And what is perhaps more important still—only thus can we explain his powerlessness to respond in any vital way to the new ideas of science and philosophy. Because the paralysis of faith has gone much deeper than the level of the intellect, the changes in the merely intellectual atmosphere are as yet of such little effect. In other words, the materialization of life has eaten so deeply into our capacity for faith that the great masses of men are powerless to respond to a non-materialistic philosophy.

IV

It is of the utmost importance, I think, that we moralists and religionists should understand just how this paralysis of faith has come about—the progressive inhibitions by which men's spiritual initiatives have been arrested. Only thus can we hope that these inhibitions may be removed.

First of all, there is still with us the post-war mind. Like many of you, I feel that the present generation should stop using this alibi. But the fact is that the post-war mind is still with us and is something that we find it extremely hard to rid ourselves of. I should put it this way. Men's souls received a greater shock than we have yet realized—especially the impressionable souls of the youth of the time. They received an overwhelming impression of futility, evil and unreason. It was an emotional impression, to be sure, but for that very reason, all the deeper.

Men must, however, rationalize their emotions and this they proceeded to do. So they immediately picked out from the world of scientific ideas and theory all those phrases and current beliefs that would fit into this feeling of unreason.

The scientific phrases they rolled under their tongues! "The struggle for existence," "the survival of the fittest," "the running down of the universe!" There were scientists who told them that the universe is an accident and that its days are numbered, that the world is irrational and working towards an irrational end. It is astonishing how much they enjoyed those views. As the naturalistic novelist and artist selected the baser aspects of life, and cried: Ah ha! We will tear the mask from life—show you how rotten it all really is, so men picked from science those theories which ministered to their sense of the irrational. We will tear the mask from the universe and show how stupid and futile the whole thing is!

Now, of course, there have always been scientists who believed those things. But there were many more who did not. The important point is that the true scientists have always recognized them as not facts but theories—that the premises on which those theories were erected are doubtful, if no longer not actually untenable. But not so the modern spiritual hypochondriac. If you try to point out to him the changing position of science on those questions, he looks at you as though you were trying to take something precious from him, much as the physical hypochondriac does when you try to prove that there is nothing wrong with him.

My contention then is that the present unbelief and irreligion is primarily moral and only secondarily intellectual. There have been acids of modernity eating at man's faith, but those acids have been secreted by life rather than by science. They are partly scientific but only partly so. It is not so much any mechanism of science, as the mechanization of life. Not so much any unreason in the universe, revealed by science and philosophy, as the unreason which he finds in his own daily life—economic, political and personal.

I feel that this last point cannot be too much stressed. This overwhelming sense of unreason in life is the ground tone of the modern world. It is said that if you scratch a Russian, you will find a Tartar. I think it may also be said that if you scratch a typically modern man anywhere, you will find an irrationalist. And this, despite the fact that, like the builders of the Tower of Babel, he goes on building his intellectual and rational structures—of science, industry and State—ever higher and higher; despite the fact that this very reason, which he distrusts, he feels to be his only good.

Men find no meaning in the world—this I have no hesitation in saying—because they find no fundamental meaning in their own lives and their own activities. The universe is without a living spirit because they find no living spirit in themselves. They have lost their faith in God because, temporarily at least, they have lost their faith in man. I should put it in this way. For some generations now man has been trying to decide whether he is merely a high-grade simian or a son of God. More philosophically put, he has been trying to decide whether his intelligence, reason, and all their values, are really merely biological products or adaptations, or whether they have a transcendental—more than merely natural—status and meaning. If he is coming to think of himself more and more as an animal, it is, I think, in the first instance because the life about him appears to be more and more jungle life, more and more the play of irrational forces.

The modern man's sense of unreason is then primarily moral, but it is not wholly so. It has assimilated to itself certain dogmas of Victorian science, and thereby created an amalgam of emotion and intellect which is extraordinarily difficult to break up. It is, I repeat, this amalgam of emotion and science, the dogmas of practice associating themselves with the dogmas of science, which makes the mind of the ordinary man impervious to the newer ideas of science and philosophy. Men have rationalized their practice by science. The process of derationalization, although it has begun, will be a long and difficult one.

But I have spent time enough on this diagnosis of the modern soul—a diagnosis upon which so many spiritual doctors have been at work. Let me sum it up in what is to my mind the best expression of the modern mood. It is found in a statement by Theodore Dreiser, published a few years ago in *The Bookman*. Exaggerated it undoubtedly is, but I have heard its equivalent in many mouths, including those of college students:

> "I can make no comment on my work or life that holds either interest or import for me. Nor can I imagine any explanation or interpretation of any life, my own included, that would be either true, or important if true. Life is to me too much a welter and play of

inscrutable forces to permit, in my case at least, any significant comment. One may paint for one's own entertainment, and that of others, perhaps. As I see it, the utterly infinitesimal individual weaves, among the mysteries, a floss-like and wholly meaningless course, if course it be. I catch no meaning from all I have seen, and pass, quite as I came, confused and dismayed."

This, one commentator adds, is the real American Tragedy, much more than Mr. Dreiser's book by that name. To this has his naturalism brought him. But it is also the American tragedy in a much wider sense. If one has not ears to hear this deep undertone beneath all the ballyhoo of the modern world, then is he spiritually deaf indeed. If he can look into the eyes of those about him and not see this look of confusion and dismay, then surely it is because he will not see. An East Indian visitor to our shores was once asked his impression of the American people. "My chief impression," he answered, "is that they are not happy. They laugh too much."

V

The first prerequisite of any fruitful dealing with the modern soul is that we should understand it. This means a clear and cool recognition of its deep-seated sense of puzzlement, futility and dismay. On the surface this may not seem very evident.

> "Fast flows our war of mocking words, and yet
> With tears mine eyes are wet. . . ."

So runs Matthew Arnold's poem on the *Buried Life* in

which the modern soul is so admirably pictured. On the surface, epigram, paradox, and wise-crack. Underneath an emptiness often much too deep for tears.

> "For often in the world's most crowded streets
> And often in the din of strife,
> There rises an unspeakable desire
> After the knowledge of our buried life. . . ."

Thus the religious, the metaphysical instinct (for they are at bottom the same), that cannot be killed. . . .

This unspeakable desire is there and, as I believe, becoming ever more articulate. There is at least this much truth in the paradox which we so often hear—that this is really a religious age. It is religious to this extent—that it somehow feels that it ought to be religious. It feels that somehow this sense of futility and dismay cannot be the last word.

Sir Philip Gibbs is entirely right, I think, when he says, "Already many minds are aghast at the disorder, and see no hope for humanity except in a revival of faith and a return to Christian Ethics. But," he adds, "they do not see how to do it."

That is the rub. They do not see how to do it. Now surely I am not naive enough to suppose that, where so many others are at a loss, I should know what to do. Surely I am not immodest enough to suppose that I can teach you the cure of modern souls—I who have lived my life in the remote regions of philosophic thought, teach you, who have fought for men's souls in the very dust and dirt of life! Surely I have no such illusions! And yet—precisely because I have, in a sense, been above the battle, I may make some useful suggestion about this far-flung battle line. I can at least try.

My thesis, all along, has been this. The present unbelief in religion is primarily moral and only secondarily intellectual. It is quite true that, as has been said, we are not confronted with an irrational preference for immorality, but rather with a generation ridden with doubts because it does not know what it prefers and why. It does not know what the good is!

To us moralists and religionists it is incredible that this should be so. After all the years of Christian experience! After the centuries of thinking from Plato to Kant! But incredible as it seems, this is the fact. As has been so often said, it is a period of moral confusion. And we must remember from what a deep-seated and ghastly indecision this confusion has arisen. There is, I repeat, only one ultimate source of all our confusion, both intellectual and moral—the modern man's uncertainty as to whether he is merely a high grade animal or a son of God. For a long time he thought that perhaps he could be both. He has now come to feel that at bottom he must be one or the other. Until he knows what he really is, he cannot know what is his true good.

Christian ethics tells him that he is a son of God. All its ideas of good and right spring from that. He may find it hard to believe, but in that belief, lies his only cure. In any case, that is really what he wants to know. There rises in him an unspeakable desire after the knowledge of his buried life. That desire will not be gainsaid. For a generation now, that buried life has been described to him in the Freudian terms of *libido* and "suppressed desires," or by a behavioristic psychology that denies that he has any buried life at all. That period is passing. He knows now that these things are not true, or at least not the whole truth. He knows that he has suppressed desires, but he knows that they are for something quite different. He knows that he has a hidden life which is something very much more. Can he not be shown what that life is—that it is a life "hid with Christ in God"?

As I see it—and I can only tell you what I see—there is no cure for the modern soul except in an out-and-out supernatural ethics, and in an out-and-out philosophical doctrine of transcendental and absolute values. For these two are, in the last analysis, one. Relativistic and naturalistic ethics have been tried and have led only to confusion. It is for this reason that I have been following with bated breath the fortunes of the struggle in our own church on the questions of marriage and sex morals. The Bishop of St. Albans is, I think, entirely right in holding that the ethics of sex and of the family are the heart of Christian ethics. That is to my mind profoundly true philosophically, for the heart of any ethics is its view of the springs of life.

I have the deepest sense of the difficulties of these problems as affected by the conditions of modern life. I have the deepest sympathy with those of our brethren who feel so keenly the difficulties and complexities of these problems. I would be the last either to wish, or to dare, to judge the pronouncements or the legislation of the Church. But I cannot believe (and here I speak with humility) that those who would accept many of the so-called modern views on this subject have really thought the matter through. These modern proposals are, many of them, based on merely human, and ultimately naturalistic, views of man and of man's life in the world. Christian morals can be based only on supernaturalistic premises, on the assumption that man is primarily a son of God. Whatever our indecision here—I cannot feel otherwise—it is really but part of our deeper indecision, as to what we really are.

Those who stand for a supernatural ethics, need have no fear, I think, from the intellectual point of view. Modernism in morals, as elsewhere, has come to an impasse and the return journey is beginning. There are many signs which indicate the way the wind is blowing. A veteran observer of the literary weather has recently said that "the most extraordinary phenomenon of American literature is the complete bankruptcy of the naturalistic movement." This bankruptcy, if it is a fact, and I believe that it is, is but a symptom of a similar bankruptcy in the higher altitudes of philosophy. One thing the modern mind is coming to see ever more clearly. Even Mr. Bernard Shaw sees that Darwinian naturalism has brought us, as he says, "to the brink of a bottomless pit." But there is something else that we are coming to see. Man, to be man, that is to be even human, must live by values which are higher than any deducible from nature. Man has intuitive glimpses of a higher reality beyond the flux and flow of nature. On the basis of these glimpses, he is enabled to form a code of values which is opposed to nature and therefore humane.

This is the thesis of that significant book, *Humanism and America.* In one form or another, it is also the thesis of a large part of more recent philosophical thought. Is not one more step inevitable? To be humane in any significant sense is to be beyond nature. To be beyond nature, in any significant sense, means to be supernatural. Merely to be values—at all—must not these ideas have their origin and their consummation in the Divine?

This also many are logical enough to see. Differ as they may and do, on many concrete issues of religion and philosophy, these humanists agree that a really humanistic view of man and religion are inseparable. Irving Babbitt came to call himself a supernaturalist, and Paul Elmer More to insist that the Christian notion of man is the only really human notion, while Dr. Castiello, the Jesuit from the other side of the fence, calls his book "A Humane Psychology of Education."

VI

The present unbelief and irreligion is primarily moral. The cure of modern souls must therefore be primarily moral. Only a doctrine of absolute moral values, such as is enshrined in the Christian ethics, can bring light and clarity into the manifold confusions of our age. But, as I have suggested all along, there is more to the situation than this. It is also partly intellectual. The modern man has rationalized his unbelief by means of a naturalistic science and an irrational philosophy. It can be derationalized only through science and philosophy.

It is at this point that the present situation in science and philosophy is of the utmost significance in the cure of modern souls. It may be accepted as certain that in the last decades the intellectual backgrounds of our spiritual life have undergone a more radical change than any perhaps since the Copernican revolution. In a *Survey of Fifty Years of Science*, Professor Henry Fairfield Osborne closed with this remark: "In my time, I have seen the materialists deny the very existence of all spirituality and now Science turns backwards—I should say forwards—and says there is something outside matter." This turning backwards, or forwards, for it is in a sense both, is the outstanding feature of recent scientific thought.

This is not the place to enter into the details of this tremendous change—to indicate step by step how it has all come about. How it is that modern physics has given the death-blow to a materialistic and mechanistic world view; how it is that the overwhelming tendency is now against reducing life and mind to matter; why, we are told by physicist after physicist—by an Eddington, a Sir James Jeans, a Weyl, and numerous others—that reality is coming to appear more and more as ultimately intelligence and mind. Nor is this the place—although it is perhaps the most important point of all—to indicate the newer views of the nature and limits of science itself—its purely relative and symbolic character. The significant thing for us is that this turning backwards or forwards, of which Professor Osborne speaks, is a basal fact of modern culture.

And what is true of science is even truer in the realms of philosophy. The "Idealistic Revolt Against Science", of which the Italian philosopher Alliotta wrote some years ago, has been gaining in strength from year to year. As a British philosopher not long ago wrote in the *Nation-Athenaeum*, "Philosophy is at this moment at the beginning of a reaction against a reaction". After describing the reaction of the twentieth century, which gave rise to various naturalisms such as Pragmatism and the New Realism, he continues,

> "This reaction has now spent itself. Brilliantly critical as its exponents are admitted to be, this philosophy of revolt has grown progressively more complex and pointless. Philosophy, it is felt, cannot go on like this. And so the systems are coming back again, and the latest writers on philosophy show a tendency to take the gods of their grandfathers off the shelf on which their fathers had placed them."

This characterization of the situation is profoundly true. Even in this country one can feel the beginning of this reaction. If we turn our eyes abroad, the situation becomes even clearer. To France—where the religion of science and scientific philosophy, so called, has long spent itself, where a philosophy of "Intuition" has set limits to a philosophy of science, and where a reaction to religion—even to Catholic ways of thinking—is a distinctive feature of the higher intellectual life. To England—where, too, the naturalistic movement, even in the hands of so good a propagandist as Russell, is showing itself to be the pointless and unintelligible thing it is, and where, as Professor Muirhead says, a philosophy of values is developing which is bringing men back to the clearer and deeper insights of traditional philosophy.

This is a significant situation for us men of religion. But woe unto us if we misinterpret and misuse this situation. Chesterton said that "men have discovered that science is a hollow sham and are tumbling over themselves coming back to religion". If there is this great return to religion, I have yet to discover it. Nor have men discovered that science is a hollow sham, for it is not that. Because science itself is coming to see that much which was thought of as dogmatic certainty is speculation, and much which was considered literal fact, is symbolic picture, it does not follow that it is wholly untrue. It is attitudes such as Chesterton's that have compromised the relations of science and religion from the beginning. There is no need for us to repeat those ancient errors.

Of one thing, however, we men of religion may be sure, and may make the basis of the cure of modern souls. Modern critical science and philosophy have, once for all, broken up the scientific dogmas of the preceding decades—its mechanism, its behaviorism, and its irrationalism. The derationalization of the dogmas with which the spiritual and moral life has been bound up has begun; the amalgam of intellect and emotion is breaking up. It is for us to carry on that work to the best of our powers.

It is true that the intellectual life of the great masses of men is still lived among the conceptions of the 19th century science. All the writers that of late have most influenced the popular mind still live among those ideas. There is no question that the influence of such men is passing, but it is still strong. Men of religion must simply know more real science and philosophy than do popular purveyors of pseudo-science. We must challenge their dogmas and ridicule their pretensions.

But the task of the Church in the present situation is a greater one than this. It must teach not only religion but religious philosophy. The period which saw the separation of faith from intellect, of religion from theology and philosophy, is passing. Men no longer say, "The important thing is to believe; it does not matter what you believe". They are coming to see, what Coleridge saw long ago, that religion is "covert metaphysics". It is simply a matter of life and death that it shall have an adequate metaphysic. Does anyone doubt the dire necessity of this? Christianity is a way of life, someone says, not a philosophy. I answer: it is the transcendent way of life that it is, only because it has a transcendentally significant philosophy of life and of the universe in which our life is lived. Why our confusion in morals? Because men do not know what they really are. Why this deep-seated puzzlement and dismay? Because men cannot see the reason at the heart of the world, the transcendent reason which St. Augustine called "God's first-born son", and which he and St. Thomas, and all the great Christian thinkers, have recognized as the very essence of Deity. In a real sense (and I say it with all care and circumspection) the cure of the modern soul is in the hands of the Christian philosopher.

VII

It is most important that this should not be misunderstood. I am convinced, to be sure, that much of the religious activity of the next decades must be intellectual and philosophical in character. Not because religion is primarily an intellectual matter. It is a much deeper thing than that; but religion is inevitably intellectual for all that, and, for the time being at least, for reasons that are evident, the intellectual aspect must be in the ascendancy of importance. Nor am I advocating, as might be supposed, the point of view of the so-called liberals or modernists in religion. It is really something quite different that I have in mind, as different as different can possibly be.

The most fatal thing about the religious thought of the last half century has been just this so-called liberalism, with its morbid feeling of the necessity of squaring the intuitions and dogmas of religion with the latest pronouncements of science, whether physical, biological or psychological. As a result, it has not only tied up religion with ephemeral scientific hypotheses, but also with the most gross sort of popular exaggerations and errors. But it did worse than that. Often, without knowing it, it accepted a pure naturalism which in the end is bound to extinguish all religion. Whatever else modernism in religion has been—in the details of its various positions—its fundamental motive has been awe of science and scientific method—its fundamental premise the primacy of the scientific point of view. Signs are everywhere multiplying that modernism in religion has come to an impasse. It not only empties churches; it makes it next to impossible for people to believe in anything or anybody.

This much, I think, is settled. The modern mind can no longer adopt any of the substitutes for supernatural religion—or any of the synthetic religions of the Victorian epoch. It has, as Mr. Lippmann says, seen through them all. Even the undergraduate mind, as I know it, has to a large degree settled that question. The truth is that full, rich, supernatural religion—or nothing—is rapidly becoming the necessary alternative of the really modern man.

But here again I would not be misunderstood. Surely the entire drift of what I have had to say is in the direction of emphasizing the intellectual element in religion. I am a modern man, and surely I should not want to detach myself from the intellectual life of the present and live in the Middle Ages, however great those ages were. No, my point is quite a different one. The modern man is coming to see through religious modernism because he is coming to see that its premises are a pure naturalism—even if some of its leaders have not always known it—and that, on these premises, religious humanism, or a religion without a God—if such a thing is possible—is the only conclusion. For modernism, religious ideas are wholly symbolic, but they are symbolic only of human and moral values. For supernatural religion these ideas are also in part symbolic, but they are symbols of great ultimate metaphysical realities. That is the great—the tremendous—difference.

Nor need we men of religion fear intellectually to insist upon this tremendous difference—a difference which determines the line between supernaturalism and a pure naturalism.

For it is precisely the philosophers, and the more philosophical scientists, that are pointing out to us the weakness of the premises of religious modernism. Professor Whitehead has said that the time has come when philosophy need no longer go to science with its hat in its hands. What he says of philosophy he says also of religion. Professor Eddington has deprecated the tendencies of what is called liberal religion, to seek to translate the dogmas of religion into scientific terms. He does so, not only because he sees that these dogmas lose much, if not all, their meaning, when thus translated, but much more because he sees that they deal with a more ultimate aspect of reality than do the symbols of science. What has been called modernism in religion has in other words committed itself to a doctrine of the primacy of science, and to views of science which themselves cannot now be maintained—and the ground is being cut from under its feet.

Men are coming more and more to see these things, I believe. For this reason what we call the Catholic position, and the philosophy that goes with it, interests them again. In the undergraduate publication to which I referred, the writer insists that the alternative is definitely between Catholicism and humanism. Dean Weigel at the Yale Divinity School, in an important address lately delivered, denies explicitly that this alternative is forced upon us, and makes an eloquent plea for "the intermediate position of historic Protestantism." But the mere fact that such an eminent man feels he must make that denial is symptomatic of much in present-day thought.

VIII

Those who are concerned with the cure of souls are familiar with the idea of battling with the forces of darkness and evil for a human soul. This situation is as real today as it ever was in the period of the so-called Dark Ages, when there was a literal devil with whom the battle could be literally joined. But how much more difficult the battle is today!

For one thing, men must be persuaded that they have souls—immortal souls; that they are really human. Men have been dehumanized by the experiences of the last decades. It is hard for them to get their humanity back again. They will have to learn again the authentic quality of human values—that lust is not love, that moral obligation is not merely taboo, that beauty is not merely nervous thrill, that the will-to-power is not morality and, finally, that knowledge is something more than mere utility. When they have relearned these things, they will know that they have souls; but what a task to relearn them!

When they really know again that they have souls, they will also know that there is a God. When they once really believe in man, they will also believe in God. When they again believe in the dignity and honor with which man has been crowned, his place in the hierarchy of values, they will again know that he is a little lower than the angels and is a son of God. To know what man really is, is to know also that there must be angelic powers, and, above all, a God who is his Father. The Christian Church is now fighting for the honor and dignity of man.

It is not for me to tell the Church how to fight this battle—how to win men, how to reconcile them unto themselves and ultimately unto God. The Church has weapons that I know little of—special stores of grace, of skill and tact, a special guidance by the Holy Spirit that is not mine. All that I have attempted, have indeed dared to attempt, is to suggest a background from which certain special problems may be viewed. I am, as it were, a watchman—one who from one part of a far-flung battle line, the intellectual part, may perhaps tell something of what I think the signs of battle are. "Watchman, tell us of the night". I have told something of the night—perhaps too much. I hope I have also been able to tell something of what the signs of promise are. For me these signs of promise are very real. I am sure my intellectual ears do not deceive me, that my spiritual senses are not playing me false. I hope that I have been able to convey something of my confidence.

IV

DOGMA, SCIENCE AND POETRY

by

Frederick Albert Pottle

Frederick Albert Pottle is Professor of English in Yale University and Fellow of Davenport College in the same. He was an undergraduate at Colby College and holds from Yale degrees of Master of Arts and Doctor of Philosophy. Glasgow University has honored him by making him a Doctor of Laws. In succession to the late Geoffrey Scott, he has become Editor of the private papers of James Boswell.

Few people nowadays really like dogma. Mr. T. E. Hulme once said that he accepted the sentiment of the Church for the sake of the dogma, thereby implying that he had a natural appetite for dogma and a natural repugnance to sentiment. He was probably sincere, but the statement on most men's lips would rightly be regarded as a paradox, for the prevailing temper of our times is favorable to religious sentiment of all kinds and unfavorable to dogma. We instinctively like the exalted feelings associated with the practice or contemplation of religion. To nearly all of us, no matter how much we believe in it, dogma presents grave and recurring difficulty.

Science and art being recognized and respectable categories, we try to escape from our difficulty by bringing dogma in under one or the other. Clergymen who respect science try to save dogma by linking it to physics. Scientists who respect religion vindicate its dogma by equating it with poetry. The result of either tactic is to destroy dogma altogether. The view which I have taken in what follows is that dogma is most important and must be preserved; and that in order to preserve it we must know in what it differs from science and from poetry.

If we oppose the attempt to save dogma by making it a department of science, we would seem to be forced to defend the opposed thesis that dogma has nothing whatever to do with science, is not concerned with it, does not touch it at any point. We must be careful not to allow ourselves to take that stand without some qualification, for it has the look of pure obscurantism. Christian dogmas, by and large, are autonomous with regard to science; but science does impinge upon them in one area which is of vital importance.

I

Science is naturalistic in its scope; dogma is not. If we are to understand that, we must pause and define what we mean by the term "nature".[1] Nature, in the widest sense, is everything that exists or has being, as it is in itself, not as it appears in the constructions of a human mind. Science postulates nature in this sense, but does not profess to know anything about it. If there be a God, He is part of nature in this widest definition.

In the second and more restricted sense, nature is all that is given to (*data*), or, as Kant more truly perceived, made by (*facta*) the human mind. We are not passive machines which nature, in the first sense, operates. Nature makes impressions on us. From these impressions the mind *constructs* the world as we know it. Color, we are aware, is not a quality of an object

[1] The following analysis of the four meanings of the term "Nature" owes a great deal to Mr. I. A. Richards, *Coleridge on Imagination*, pp. 157-8.

but a sensation in the brain. There is something in the object capable of absorbing a portion of the spectrum when white light falls on it; the unabsorbed rays are reflected on the retina, and the resulting sensation in the brain we call "red." What the something in the object which is responsible for this is *in itself*, we have no way of knowing. We must bring in light and the human eye before we learn anything about it at all.

In the same way it is obvious that sounds are not "things in themselves", but sensations in the brain. It is not so obvious that volume and mass as we perceive them in bodies are not qualities of things in themselves. A little reflection, however, will show that, like color and sound, they too are constructions of our minds, built up from the sense of touch and from muscular sensations.

We can go on to still more disquieting conclusions. Space and time, which seem so completely independent of humanity, are not qualities of things in themselves but mental categories, frames into which the *facta* of experience must be fitted before they make any kind of sense.[2]

Nature in the second meaning mentioned above is a selection made from nature in this first meaning of

[2] My illustrations of *facta* in this section happen all to be presented in terms of a materialistic philosophy, but it would be a mistake to suppose that all the *facta* of experience are *necessarily* of a sort to be included in a materialistic or physiological description. If there be a God, He will still remain in this definition of nature, and He may be known to the human mind through the recognized senses or by other means. The pronouncement that the senses recognized by science are the *only* avenues of knowledge of what exists is what I shall call hereafter a "nothing-but fallacy."

the word. It is that portion of existing things which the human mind is capable of apprehending. Rather, it is the sum of the constructions which the human mind puts upon things so apprehended.

Nature in a third, and still more restricted, meaning is that portion of nature in the second sense on which all man are agreed insofar as they are sane and normal. It is the realm of "natural law". It is the part of nature which is of the greatest *immediate* importance, for we must observe its ways if we are to live at all. Men may not agree upon a point in theology or upon the value of a given piece of poetry. They do agree that if you touch fire, you will be burned; that if you are long submerged in water, you will drown; that if you leap from a tall building, you will be dashed to pieces. This is the realm of science, in the gross or popular sense. It is of *general* application, and takes from individual experience only so much as is applicable to all men. In most problems that face mankind, it has no room for the individual.[3]

The Christian God, a reality not apprehended by all men in an invariable fashion, is excluded from "nature" at exactly this point. When we speak of a philosophy or method as "materialistic", "mechanistic", or "naturalistic", we are using an imperfect nomenclature to indicate that the conception of nature em-

[3] E.g. the science of statistics enables a life-insurance company to assign a predicted life-span to me at any age, and to insure me for such an annual premium as will enable the company *in its transactions as a whole* to make a profit. But this gives me no assurance that I shall live ten days after I take out the policy.

ployed excludes everything not found in nature *in this third sense.*

Nature in the fourth sense is a still narrower selection from nature in the second sense, and consists of only so much of Sense III as theoretical science needs for its constructions. Matter here loses its "common sense" attributes of density, color, mass, etc., and becomes a swarm of invisible electric particles. Science here tends towards the austere and completely abstract constructions of mathematics. There are undoubtedly metaphysical assumptions underlying this kind of science, but since the materials on which they operate are those of nature in Sense III, they are incapable of being developed into theology. And this final sort of "nature", or *theoretical* science, rests on unprovable postulates most readily illustrated by the axioms in geometry.

II

What precedes has been dull reading; but I hope that all those who propose to follow me through the remainder of this essay have tried to peruse it. We constantly meet the statement that science is a selection, or abstraction, from the fulness of reality. My experience indicates that that phrase is pretty much meaningless until one has been conducted through some such scheme as that which I have outlined, and has seen the rich welter of human experience—its hopes, its fears, its loves, its ecstasies, its despairs, its colors, its tones, its feeling—all stripped down to the beautifully clear, but cold and impersonal, constructions of theoretical science.

The selection does not (and this is important) proceed by mapping off certain areas and excluding them as beyond the domain of science. It proceeds rather by a rarefication or a stripping down. If we think of nature in Sense II as a square, nature in Sense III is not a smaller square marked off within its boundaries. The domain of theoretical science is coextensive with all human experience, but within that area it ignores all but a small fraction of what it finds.

Science achieves its beautiful clarity and precision by deliberately excluding, at the very beginning, everything that will not fit into the final pattern. I am not surprised when laymen with no training in science are depressed by the triumphant emergence of a scientist from an argument in which everything is explained and God left out; but I am indeed surprised when I occasionally see scientists themselves exhilarated by such tugging at their boot-straps. Of course God is left out. He was left out by definition, at the very outset. There can be a "scientific" description, or explanation, of practically anything; but no one should suppose that such an explanation—though true—exhausts the object.

Yet we must avoid setting boundaries to the scientific method and saying, "Up to this point science may operate, but no further". There are no such boundaries. The proper procedure is not to deny the right of science to push its inquiries out to any limits it chooses, but to evaluate the results of its inquiries in terms of our *total* experience. Not, "This is false," but, "This seems to contain no logical fallacy, *but what of it?*"

Arguments from science to religious sanctions are very dangerous and should invariably be avoided by those who have not had a considerable training in science. In spite of what one reads in popular books on religion, the theory of relativity makes belief in God no easier than it was before. It also makes it no harder. It just has nothing to do with belief in God. Electricity has nothing to do with the doctrine of the Communion of Saints. The arrogance of irreligious science is often blamed in our time. The devout should be quite as much concerned with the ignorant use of popular science in theological discussion.

Christian theology very obviously rests on unprovable postulates—the statements of the Creed. Many Christians worry constantly over the fact that they are unprovable. Theoretical science also rests on unprovable postulates, but few people worry about them. They seem, as we say, "self-evident." Why is this?

It is, I think, because of the operation of what I may call "mental climate". Every age has its mental climate, the effect of which is to make men unconscious of the postulates they make in that field of endeavor to which the mental climate is favorable. The mental climate of the modern world is favorable to the development of theoretical science. Hence with no hesitation or anxiety we make the postulates demanded by science. Furthermore, the effect of mental climate is to cause us to arrogate for one (and only one) kind of human thought, the function of dealing with "truth" or "reality". The natural temper of our minds now is scientific. Without being taught to do so, we assign all "truth" to the province of science. Whatever science cannot manipulate we feel to be unreal or untrue.

Now, we have plenty of evidence that there have been eras during which the mental climate was favorable to metaphysics and theology, and unfavorable to natural science. In this connection, the Gnostic heresy, at the very beginning of the Christian church, is most enlightening. The Gnostics were repelled by the historical element in Christianity, and repudiated it in favor of a purely metaphysical and mystical belief.

Or consider the "science" of the Middle Ages, in which the passion for placing everything in the framework of Christian theology completely dominated the will to collect, to analyze and to experiment. Every text of Scripture, no matter how prosaic a statement of historical fact, was given not one, but three allegorical meanings. Every object in nature had a spiritual significance, more important than its material content.

The bestiaries are the natural-history texts of the period. In them purely fabulous animals such as the unicorn and the onocentaur are presented as seriously as the goat or the stag, and hardly a real animal escapes without fabulous traits. The elephant has only one joint in his legs and must sleep leaning against a tree; to capture him you saw the tree partly through. Once he has fallen on his side, he cannot get up again. The weasel is bisexual; it impregnates itself in the mouth and the young are born through the ear. And so on. How could men be content to remain so ignorant of ascertainable facts? Because they were "making sense" of nature in a framework (the theological) which interested them more than the scientific. Every one of those animals had a theological meaning. They were types of Christ, Adam, Eve, the Blessed Virgin, the Devil, etc. What the author was concerned with was the ingenious exposition of the allegory inherent in the traits of the animals. Those traits he was content to take on hearsay.

Let us not be too quick to smile at him. Our own solemn satisfaction with attempts to explain the entire range of existence in terms of a materialistic philosophy are probably just as absurd. The view now current that *our* mental climate came to us by a long and painful growth in which the race passed from mental adolescence to mental maturity is probably self-flattery. Every previous age has likewise made the calm assumption that *its* mental climate represented mental maturity, and apparently with just as good reason.

History rather suggests that the scientific temper is not the result of a gradual and progressive growth of the mind, but that it came suddenly and inexplicably by a shift of mental organization, and that it may depart as suddenly and inexplicably. Where is the evidence of a gradual development of the scientific temper from Aristotle to Archimedes to Francis Bacon and Galileo? Is it not clear that the ancient

Greeks could have made every discovery in science on which we pride ourselves, if they had thought it worth while?

One remembers that famous quotation from Seneca, which Macaulay quotes so appositely in his essay on Bacon:

> "In my own time, there have been inventions of this sort, transparent windows, tubes for diffusing warmth equally through all parts of a building, shorthand, which has been carried to such a perfection that a writer can keep pace with the most rapid speaker. But the inventing of such things is drudgery for the lowest slaves; philosophy lies deeper. It is not her office to teach men how to use their hands. The object of her lessons is to form the soul."[4]

The fact is that Aristotle (in his biological work, not in his metaphysics) and Archimedes were not typical of Greek mentality as a whole, which held experimentation in contempt as involving manual labor, and devoted itself whole-heartedly to only one science—mathematics. All through the Middle Ages a different mental climate reigned. Then suddenly—overnight as it were—the modern temper was born. There has been no real progression in it since Galileo; only an enormously fruitful extension of it in human life.

Everyone, I suppose, has heard something about sound-shifts in language, but not everyone realizes

[4] See also Plotinus: "For who that is strong enough to meditate upon the original turns by choice to its phantasm? Witness the circumstance that among children it is the dunces who betake themselves to the crafts and manual employments, because they are not competent to learning and meditation" (*Enn.* III. viii. 4, trans. E. R. Dodds).

how sudden and mysterious those shifts were. At a given moment in history, dated by linguists with some accuracy, the parent Germanic language, which up to that time had preserved approximately the same consonant scheme as its sister tongues–Sanskrit, Latin, Greek, and the Celtic languages–suddenly suffered a thorough-going change. The sound represented by *p* became *f;* that represented by *t* became *th*; that represented by *k* became the sound written *ch* in German. Then *b*, *d*, *g* became *p*, *t*, *k*. The effect was totally to disguise the kinship of English, Dutch, German, and the Scandinavian tongues with the other Indo-European languages.

Take a more recent illustration from English. As late as the middle of the fourteenth century, the long vowels in English bore approximately the same relation to the characters used to represent them as they do at present in Italian, French or German. That is, the series *ā*, *ē*, *ī*, *ō*, *ū*, would have been pronounced about the same by an Englishman or by an Italian. Before the middle of the fifteenth century, these sounds had all shifted according to a regular pattern. *Ā* became *ō*, *ō* became *ū*, *ū* became *au*, *ē* became *ī*, *ī* became *ai*. Though the sounds have changed, the spellings were in most cases not altered; hence the great discrepancy of values in the English and Continental alphabets. The most interesting things about these shifts are these: first, they took place during a sharply defined period of time, before and after which the sounds in question show no tendency to shift; and second, nobody knows why they happened.

I am suggesting that the whole shift from the medieval to the modern temper was probably analogous. Man is a complex of many forces, held in precarious equilibrium during what we call an "age". But the equilibrium tends always to be broken. When it is broken, the system rushes into a new (and equally precarious) stabilization.

There are two principles which we need to master and to practice constantly. The first is very simple and is clear to anyone the instant it is pointed out; the other is much more difficult, though to our children it will probably be a commonplace.

To begin with the easy one: science of today (science of yesterday was even worse) is often guilty of what someone has called the "nothing-but fallacy"—that is, of consciously or unconsciously assuming that a scientific description of an object exhausts it. Love between man and woman can be explained in terms of glandular secretions, and the explanation will be true. It is then assumed that "love is *nothing but* glands", which is a fallacy. Other examples will readily occur: "a rainbow is nothing but sunlight refracted by raindrops"; "poetry is nothing but the association of images"; "history is nothing but the operation of economic forces"—etc., etc.

As we have seen, science achieves its precision and coherence by rigorous *selection* from the matter of experience. It excludes by definition nine-tenths of any individual experience. Its constructions are inevitably mechanistic because it has sorted over its materials at the outset and has rejected all those that will not fit into a mechanistic scheme.

Now, our mental climate causes us to assume that the materials which it rejects are not "real". They are just as real as the others, and often, so far as you and I are concerned, of greater importance. Science is never in a position to claim totality. After the scientist has finished, there is just as much room as before for a different or complementary description. Both may be true, though no logic can reconcile them.

That brings me to the second principle. I follow Mr. T. E. Hulme in calling it the principle of discontinuity. Theology and science are not different areas of a single *continuum*, like the bands of long and short waves in the spectrum. They are discontinuous. They do not operate in different territories, which may be bridged by logic. They operate in the same territory, but they are logically irreconcilable.

It requires a good deal of a mental wrench to grasp this notion, and I doubt if our generation will ever be at home in it. The scientists take to it much more readily than the rest of us. We *know* instinctively that the Aristotelian logic of cause and effect and the Euclidean geometry are of the essence of things. When we say that a straight line is the shortest distance between two points, or that through a given point in a plane only one parallel to a given line can be drawn, we do not feel in the least as though we were postulating something. But we are. Both statements are incapable of proof, and it is only habit and mental climate which makes them seem "self-evident".

Our scientists now have another series of geometries based on such equally legitimate assumptions as that a curved line is the shortest distance between two points and that through a given point in a plane any number of parallels can be drawn. Or again: Newton believed light to be made up of particles; later science decided that it was a wave motion. Now it is made up of particles on Monday, Wednesday and Friday, but is a wave motion on Tuesday, Thursday and Saturday.[5]

The corpuscular theory and the wave theory are not modifications of a single hypothesis; they are logically irreconcilable, discontinuous. *But they both work*. By using the corpuscular theory on certain occasions, the scientist can "make sense" of a mass of data which the wave theory is impotent to organize, and can make predictions which experiment verifies. Some of my scientific friends to whom I have talked are confident that the logical difficulties will be resolved ultimately by yet another theory. I suspect that the new theory will probably be no more than a Greek name for the anomaly. Many difficulties seem to disappear as soon as we have a name for them. What the scientists have arrived at (and they should be proud of having arrived at it before the rest of us), is the principle of discontinuity.

In short, the universe can be embraced by no single human system of thought—nor, for that matter, by all

[5] This rather flippant characterization I heard from the late E. E. Slosson, and some more of the illustration in this portion may be unconscious recollection either of his lecture or one of his books, which I read many years ago.

of them together. The notion that science is a caterpillar on the edge of the leaf of the universe, settling down to the comfortable job of eating and digesting it all, is no less fantastic than the medieval belief that the whole universe could be comprehended within the framework of theology. Science is a glorious demonstration of the powers of the human mind, and our scientific constructions are undoubtedly the greatest achievement of this age; but science does not make religious dogma either fatuous or unnecessary.

The elements of experience are like pieces of a huge jigsaw puzzle, thrown out before us on a table. As we sort them over, we despair of fitting them into a single pattern. But little by little, we find that we can select one sort of pieces that *will* make a pattern, and another sort that will make another pattern. Finally we can account for a good many of the pieces. That is the best we can expect. For better or for worse, we must face the difficult position of having, treasuring, and using discontinuous systems which long experience has shown to be necessary to a really abundant life.

I have spoken of science and dogma as being "irreconcilable by logic". By that I do not mean that theology is illogical; rather that neither system, no matter how far extended, will ever include the other. They are not so much hostile as incommensurate. I know that many thoughtful people who are attracted to the Catholic position feel that they cannot accept it because it is "repugnant to reason". Actually, the dogmas to which they object usually have nothing to do with reason, being postulates prior to any logical construction. The logic of Catholicism, when it is really a question of logic, is generally held, even by unbelievers, to be very impressive. What the statement "repugnant to reason" really means is that the postulates are felt to be contradictory to the modern or scientific spirit. And so they are, though I should prefer to say "disparate with" rather than "contradictory to". We cannot prove them. Neither can we prove the axioms of science. It is merely our mental climate that makes us acutely aware of the postulates in theology and unconscious of those in science.

We must not expect to dwell in orthodox Christianity without some mental strain. If we examine the first articles of the Nicene Creed, we shall at once agree that they are not "scientific." Take one point that is particularly illuminating: Jesus Christ is said to have been begotten of His Father "before all worlds." Now science knows nothing of any event that happened "before all worlds". It may assign fantastic antiquity to an event; but it can never say, "This event happened out of all time." The statement that God the Father made all things by the Son can never be brought within the domain of science. Science assumes its kind of world as existing to begin with. It knows nothing of how it came into being.

Yet we must be cautious when we say that science "has nothing to do" with Christian dogma. Christianity is an historical religion, and the whole central portion of the Creed consists of statements that either are true in the scientific sense or are not true in any sense at all.

That Jesus Christ came down from Heaven for us men and for our salvation, and that He was incarnate by the Holy Ghost, are statements which science must decline to investigate. But that He was born of a virgin, that He suffered under Pontius Pilate, was crucified, dead, and buried; that after being dead three days He returned to life again—those statements are entirely in the domain of science.

Science, of course, cannot now actually investigate the alleged virgin birth of Christ, nor His physical resurrection; but as those are events which, if they happened at all, happened within the framework of science's own kind of nature, it can legitimately subject them to its own kind of interpretation. The conclusion is inevitable because of the restriction of the premises. Since we have no scientifically authenticated record of a human being born without a human father, since we have no scientifically authenticated record of a human being who rose from the dead—or to change the language, since our experimental generalizations indicate overwhelmingly that the sexual union of father and mother is necessary for the procreation of a child and that the functions of life are not restored after sufficient time has elapsed for *rigor mortis* to ensue, there is (speaking scientifically), a very high degree of probability that these events did not take place as the Creed says they did.

Notice that I say "a very high degree of probability." In the rough and ready generalizations of everyday life, we would say, "It is certain that these events did not take place." That is not scientific. True science must envisage the possibility of even such extraordinary happenings. Some of the lower animals (e.g. frogs) are, or may be, produced from unfertilized ova. Recent experimentation with dogs has shown that life can be restored after a longer period of "death" than was formerly thought possible. But all this is not of the slightest comfort to those who wish to buttress their theology by science. If science decided that Jesus was born of a virgin, it would classify the event as "parthenogenesis", an extremely rare but quite *natural* occurrence. *From naturalistic premises you cannot arrive at supernatural sanctions;* and the sooner writers on religion realize it, the better.

It is this fact—that Christian dogma, in the main wholly outside the domain of science, does impinge upon science in one crucial area—which causes dogma to present such grave difficulties. It may be some comfort to realize, however, that this state of strain is nothing new. Christian dogma has always felt that strain as purely metaphysical systems have not. I have referred to the Gnostics: how they tried to remove the strain by removing the historical element. Our tendency is to try to remove it by eliminating the supernatural element. There is no finality about either the Gnostic temper of mind or ours. The finality is in the Church and its Creed.

Our trouble springs from the fact that, being pervaded unconsciously by the scientific temper, we begin with the historical portion of the Creed and work outward. If (we say) Jesus was a man, born of a woman, who died on the cross, it is probable that He was *merely* a man, and did die; and all the rest—about the Persons of the Trinity, the Virgin-Birth, the Resurrection, the Ascension, the Last Judgment, even the Catholic and Apostolic Church—is, as Matthew Arnold uncompromisingly maintained, "*Aberglaube*", "fairy Tales", "the three Lord Shaftesburys." But nothing obliges us to take the Creed in that order; nor should we ever so take it if our interest is in religion.

We should start with the supernatural portion and come inward. *If* Jesus Christ was begotten by His Father before all worlds, *if* by Him all things were made, then there is nothing surprising in His Virgin Birth, His Resurrection, or His Ascension. That is, we should deliberately—even if we must do violence to our ordinary habits—remove the historical portion of the Creed entirely from the setting of natural science, and place it in the setting of theology, where as part of a system of religion it belongs.

In short, you cannot combine the naturalistic postulates of science with the supernatural postulates of theology. Either you must follow your naturalistic argument unflinchingly to its conclusion, with a result that you will find all the sanctions of orthodox Christianity excluded; or you must frankly accept, by an act of faith, those postulates which assign to the Church a supernatural origin and a supernatural guidance. On that basis Catholic dogma is unassailable. On any other it is entitled to no particular respect.

As I re-read this, it seems to me that in my effort to make the principle of discontinuity clear, I have over-emphasized the difficulty of living with disparate systems. Science and theology are irreconcilable by logic, but they are reconcilable in conduct. I think of the problem of living as analagous to the problem of a tight-rope walker balanced over an abyss. He leans now to one side, now to the other, instinctively, to maintain his balance, but *he gets ahead on the wire*. Of course in the mind of God all our systems are reconcilable and a unity. Their disparateness is merely the measure of our finite natures.

III

Since Christian dogma cannot be fitted into the framework of natural science, the modern mind, if it saves any of that dogma, is apt to do it by identifying dogma with poetry. It will be useful to develop some modern theories of poetry which show this tendency, together with some others that seem to me more sound.

Literature and Dogma is the title of a once famous book by Matthew Arnold; a book which is still superior, both in style and argument, to other books defending similar positions. Arnold's book is beautifully clear, because, after his habit, he eschewed everything complicated and metaphysical, and chose a rigorously positivistic standpoint. Conduct, he says, is three-fourths of life. Religion is no more–and no less–than "morality touched by emotion." The sole concern of the authors of the Old Testament was conduct, or, to use a word "touched by emotion", righteousness. The theology of the Jews was completely unspeculative. God, to the prophets, was "the Eternal, not ourselves, that makes for righteousness." The language of the major books of the Old Testament is the language of poetry, not of metaphysics. It is language "thrown out at a not fully grasped object"–language which makes no pretense of being precise. But this grand and simple religion was obscured by a vast *Aberglaube*.[6] This *Aberglaube* can be seen in such a late book as *Daniel*.

Jesus Christ restored and perfected the original message of Judaism. His concern, like that of the prophets, was with conduct, but He taught a method and revealed a secret. For Him God was no more than "the Eternal, not ourselves, that makes for righteousness". But He taught men the only successful method of being righteous. His language was the vivid language of poetry, not the language of science or of metaphysics. He was "above the heads of his followers", who interpreted as literal what he meant to be figurative. And so, almost immediately, a new *Aberglaube* arose, obscuring the message of Jesus even in the earliest records.

The result was metaphysics and dogma–all, to use Arnold's words, "fairy tales." The dogma of the Atonement is a fairy tale; the doctrine of the Trinity (which Arnold ridiculed indecently in a parable of the three Lords Shaftesbury), worse than a fairy tale. For dogma as dogma Arnold leaves no place whatever. For literature, for poetry, he had, and wished others

[6] *Anglice*, "superstition." Arnold says that he prefers the German word to the English because it has less derogatory coloring.

to have, a consuming passion. But the sooner we got rid of Christian dogma (not some dogmas, but all dogma), the better off we should be.

> "The reasons [for believing that God is a person who thinks and loves] drawn from metaphysics one dismisses with sheer satisfaction. They have convinced no one, they have given rest to no one, they have given joy to no one. People have swallowed them, people have fought over them, people have shown their ingenuity over them; but no one has ever enjoyed them. Nay, no one has ever really understood them."[7]

With poetry it is a different case.

> "The future of poetry is immense, because in poetry, where it is worthy of its high destinies, our race, as time goes on, will find an ever surer and surer stay. There is not a creed which is not shaken, not an accredited dogma which is not shown to be questionable, not a received tradition which does not threaten to dissolve. Our religion has materialized itself in the fact, in the supposed fact; it has attached its emotion to the fact, and now the fact is failing it. But for poetry the idea is everything; the rest is a world of illusion, of divine illusion.[8] Poetry attaches its emotion to the idea; the idea *is* the fact. The strongest part of our religion today is its unconscious poetry."[9]

Arnold himself (if one can trust the language of *Literature and Dogma*, and *God and the Bible*) would have found no "unconscious poetry" in such formu-

[7] *God and the Bible*, New York, 1875, pp. 104-5 (Chapter II).

[8] I do not understand this, and doubt if Arnold did. In a system which has repudiated metaphysics, what are we to make of such a phrase as "divine illusion"?

[9] The opening paragraph of *The Study of Poetry*, which leads off the *Essays in Criticism*, Second Series.

laries as the Nicene Creed or the *Quicunque vult.* In the Bible, yes—everywhere, for that is language "thrown out" at an object. But since the intent of the framers of the Creed was to use definite and precise language, he would apparently have held it in contempt. One can see, however, how his position might very easily be extended until dogma was accepted as poetry. I well remember how an intelligent woman once said to me, "I cannot say the Apostles' Creed because it is bare, bald statement of things which I do not believe. But I can recite the Nicene Creed with fervor, because it is such glorious poetry."

The proposal to substitute poetry for dogma is usually indicative of intense moral earnestness. Arnold was a strenuous and sincere moralist. Literature acquired its vast importance for him because it, and it alone, could "touch conduct with emotion." One came to the essential things in life through culture, which is knowing "the best that has been thought and said in the world." No poetry could be called supremely great unless it possessed "high seriousness."

From Arnold we may profitably turn to his slightly younger contemporary, Count Leo Tolstoi. Arnold is the better critic; Tolstoi by far the greater theorist. Indeed, Tolstoi's *What is Art* may justly be regarded as the basic work in modern theory of poetry, and one of the three or four most important books of all time in that field. Every one knows how Tolstoi, after having written the great novels on which his fame as an artist rests, underwent a religious conversion, studied and meditated for years over the problem of religion, and when he had settled that, both in theory and practice, turned with equal persistence and vigor to an examination of the problem of art. Like Arnold (and all really modern theorists) he abandons metaphysics. Art in its essence, he says, is the transmission of feeling, nothing more.

> "To evoke in oneself a feeling one has experienced, and having evoked it in oneself, then, by means of movements, lines, colors, sounds, or forms expressed in words, so to transmit the feeling that others may experience the same feeling,–that is the activity of Art."[10]

When we say that art is good, we are really making two judgments, not one.[11] Art is good (effective might be a better word) in the first sense if it succeeds in infecting others with the feeling intended–if it *does* transmit feeling. Tolstoi insists that this kind of goodness must be evaluated quantitatively. The work of art must be generally infectious, must produce its effect upon the unlettered peasant as well as upon the aristocrat. All obscure works, all works appealing only to a class, are in this sense bad art, or rather, they are "counterfeit art", not art at all. (His prime examples of counterfeit art are the operas of Wagner and the writings of the French symbolist poets.)

Art is good in the second sense if the feeling transmitted is good; and to be good it must be in accord with the best religious perception of its time. The re-

[10] *What Is Art,* Chapter V.

[11] Tolstoi calls these the "judgment of art considered apart from subject-matter" and the "judgment according to subject-matter."

ligious perception of our time is "the consciousness that our well-being, both material and spiritual, individual and collective, temporal and eternal, lies in the growth of brotherhood among all men—in their loving harmony with one another."[12] In proportion as he repudiates the orthodox sanctions of Christianity, he assigns a high place to art. "Art is not a pleasure, a solace or an amusement; art is a great matter. Art is an organ of human life, transmitting man's reasonable perception into feeling."[13] And only as man's "reasonable perception" is transformed into feeling does he do the things he should.

It is easy, because of their intense moral earnestness, to group Arnold and Tolstoi. I wish to add a third to the company: Mr. I. A. Richards. A hasty reading of his *Principles of Literary Criticism* would probably not lead one to make that association, for he has seen fit to present his system with a flippancy which belies his real seriousness. But moralist he is; and he makes for poetry claims as resounding as do Arnold and Tolstoi.

Richards' method is psychological. As one would expect, his philosophy is materialistic and his ethics utilitarian. At the base of his system lies what he believes to be a purely psychological theory of value.

[12] *What Is Art*, Chapter XVI. He by no means evades the demand for illustration. Schiller's *Robbers;* Hugo's *Les Pauvres Gens* and *Les Misérables*; Dickens' *Tale of Two Cities*, *Christmas Carol*, *The Chimes*, and others; Harriet Beecher Stowe's *Uncle Tom's Cabin*; Dostoievsky's works generally; George Eliot's *Adam Bede* —are good art. Of his own works all are bad except *God Sees the Truth* and *The Prisoner of the Caucasus.*

[13] *What Is Art*, Chapter XX.

Metaphysical sanctions are dismissed as unnecessary. Morals are regarded as purely prudential: we do not avoid doing a thing because the Church forbids it but because, on the whole, we shall lose more by the action than we shall gain. The human mind is a systematization of impulses—or to confine ourselves to the positive expression of impulses—our minds are, at any given moment, a swarm of "appetencies", each one of which seeks its peculiar gratification. But all cannot be gratified, for the gratification of one frequently gets in the way of the gratification of another. There is inevitably a certain amount of conflict, of thwarting and frustration. "That organization which is least wasteful of human possibilities is the best."[14]

Poetry represents precisely the record of this "best" organization. "The artist is concerned with the record and perpetuation of the experiences which seem to him most worth having. . . . He is the point at which the growth of the mind shows itself. . . . His work is the ordering of what in most minds is disordered."[15] As we reproduce his experiences, we achieve better co-ordination ourselves, become saner, wiser, and happier. "The basis of morality, as Shelley insisted, is laid not by preachers but by poets."[16]

Mr. Richards' analysis of the relations between science and poetry is very interesting.[17] Both poetry and

[14] *Principles of Literary Criticism,* p. 52.

[15] *Idem,* p. 61.

[16] *Idem,* p. 62.

[17] I abstract it from one of his later books, *Coleridge on Imagination.* In the preface of this volume, he says that he is con-

science deal in "myths," a myth being "a projection of some human situation, of some co-ordination of human feeling, needs, and desires." But there is this difference: we must give unqualified belief to the myths of science, "belief" here meaning not that we think the constructions of science to be objectively and absolutely so, but that we shall always grant them "according action." "What we know as science, that we must act upon, under pain of imminent danger to our lives if we do not." On the contrary, our response in action to the myths of poetry and religion is "restricted and conditional."[18] Poems (and religious beliefs) have served their purpose when they have produced a superior co-ordination of our faculties, an attitude. A single sentence from *Principles of Literary Criticism* gives the entire system in essence:

> "The joy which is so strangely the heart of the experience [of tragedy] is not an indication that 'all's right with the world' or that 'somewhere, somehow, there is Justice'; it is an indication that all is right here and now in the nervous system."[19]

Arnold, then, regards poetry as a substitute for dogma. Richards identifies dogma (so far as it has

---

scious of having adopted no position at variance with that announced in his earlier works. It seems to me that a most significant shift of ground occurs between *Coleridge on Imagination* and the early *Science and Poetry*. This is not the place to develop it, but believing as I do that the later view is basically different from the earlier, I should not be treating Mr. Richards fairly if I took the scheme from *Science and Poetry*, as, on many grounds, I should like to do.

[18] *Coleridge on Imagination*, pp. 173-175.

[19] P. 246.

value) with poetry. Tolstoi, while keeping clear from either position, joins with them in assigning to poetry the very highest importance as a moral force, and in evaluating it by its moral content. Let us now look at two other critics who, while they have no greater respect for traditional dogma, abandon the attempt to bind art to morality.

Benedetto Croce, the great Italian historian, educator and critic, is the author of a complete philosophical system which is much too vast to be summarized in such a study as this, though it is not easy to comprehend his aesthetic theory without some knowledge of the outlines of the whole Crocean philosophy. According to him, there are four (and only four) fundamental forms of human activity—four aspects of mind: the aesthetic, the logical, the economic, and the ethical. Croce's revolutionary change is that instead of making art the apex of man's powers, he makes it the base. It is the first grade of knowledge, prior to logic, prior to morals. Matter makes its impression on mind. Mind imposes its form on matter, grasps it by direct intuition. These intuitions are completely non-reflective, individual, and particular. The mind *expresses* its intuitions, and that expression is art.

All expression is art, and all art is expression. All language is art; the difference between this essay and *Hamlet* is a quantitative, not a qualitative, difference. We all do constantly what the artist does, but our intuitions lack the coherence and complexity of his. This first grade of knowledge is presupposed in all the other grades but does not presuppose them.

Speaking theoretically, it is possible to have an aesthetic without an ethic, but it is not possible to have an ethic without an aesthetic.

Art is the intuitive knowledge of particulars. Logic is conceptual knowledge, or knowledge of the universal. All the stuff upon which it works is furnished by the aesthetic activity. Both these activities are purely theoretical, and as such are not subject to moral judgments.[20] The Practical includes two grades which bear the same relation to each other as the Aesthetic and the Logic: the Economic, which consists of particular actions useful to the individual, and the Ethical, which consists of actions based on universal concepts. The Economic underlies the Ethical, the Logic underlies the Economic, the Aesthetic underlies them all. A good deed is better than a good poem, but without poems there can be no good deeds. One cannot overemphasize in this system the primary and non-moral nature of art. It is ultimately the source of morality, but is not itself moral in any way.[21]

I shall mention one other modern critic, Mr. Max Eastman. Like Mr. Richards, he has a fondness for psychology, and like Mr. Richards he has taught college classes, but whereas Mr. Richards can adequately

[20] Not so simple as it sounds, for with Croce expression is a purely mental event. Every work of art is complete in the mind. Externalizing art by tones, pigments, letters, etc., is not an aesthetic but a practical activity. It may be necessary to restrict or prohibit the circulation of certain books, but in doing so we may often be in the position of having to say, "This is a superb work of art."

[21] Croce's system, as will be seen, has no place for religion, which he regards as imperfect philosophy.

be described as a Cambridge don, one would give a more correct notion of Mr. Eastman by calling him a poet and a journalist of radical political views. His book *The Literary Mind* is one of the most readable and entertaining works on the theory of poetry which has appeared in recent years.

He expresses the view, now becoming somewhat old-fashioned, that the onward march of science is fast destroying the claim of any kind of thought except scientific thought to be denominated knowledge. But he breaks sharply with Mr. Richards in his conception of the respective relations which science and poetry bear to conduct. Poetry in Mr. Richards' system, as we have seen, is made to bear a very heavy practical load: it disciplines us for good deeds.[22] Poetry, Mr. Eastman says, gives us the qualities of things, science indicates their uses. So far as it is "pure", poetry has nothing to do with conduct; it enables us merely to have a "heightened consciousness" of things, to feel them, to live in them. The moment we begin to organize things so as to do something about them, we cease to be aware of them. That activity is precisely science; for conduct, science is all in all.[23]

[22] Remembering always that Mr. Richards' theory of morals is purely prudential.

[23] The following passage from p. 187 of *The Literary Mind* illustrates this better than any words of mine could. Mr. Eastman has made the ingenious suggestion that "what makes us conscious of one thing rather than another, is usually some difficulty that it presents from the standpoint of our activities. . . . We can dress ourselves from top to toe without once consciously perceiving a limb or a garment, provided the garments are in their proper place, and the limbs too, and all goes well. But if something obstructs the process—if an arm will not pass through the sleeve of a coat—

Mr. Eastman has a pleasant time exposing the pretensions of the critics, professors, theologians and metaphysicians. They all indulge in "literary loose talk" in an age that has learned the difference between stating a fact and announcing an attitude. Up to about the time of Francis Bacon, literary men thought of themselves as revealers of the truth. The poet was a seer, a divine teacher. Now science has demonstrated its sole right to impart knowledge, and the field of literature is shrinking. Literary men (including all those who indulge in "literary loose talk") are being remorselessly pushed from one line of defence to another. There is no tenable line of defence. The business of the critic is to realize that the poet has nothing to do with the transmission or revelation of truth: he is concerned not with conduct but with experience. He gives us the qualities of things, not their uses. Poetry is an extension of experience, and all experience is valuable for its own sake.

I shall now, I hope with proper humility, point out my objections to these systems. Arnold seems to me an

---

then that situation automatically swims into our ken. Or suppose it has been dimly in our ken, it becomes more sharply so. It swims into the focus of attention. And as it does so the sleeve which our arm will not pass through becomes, let us say, a hole in the lining of our coat. As soon as we have perceived the experience in this way—and perhaps inwardly named it *torn lining*—the process of dressing is resumed with a correction, and may now go through to the end without further intrusion from the mind." (The identifying process here is science; the "heightened consciousness" caused by the torn lining is not poetry—for the experience is one of "practical life"—but is identical with the poetic experience except in the manner of its cause.)

example of a man carrying on by the ethical momentum of a discarded theology. His character was formed by association with his father, the intensely spiritual broad-churchman, Thomas Arnold. Without that background of training and habit he would not have arrived at his own moral earnestness. He did not get it from "culture", nor can anybody else. Secular literature, divorced from theology and dogmatic morality, will not produce it. It would be truer to say that Arnold's moral character, already formed, found partial expression in Homer, Sophocles, and the Bible.

Tolstoi made, as I believe, one contribution of permanent importance to aesthetics: he established for the first time the twofold nature of the critical act. But he substituted his own narrow and fanatical system of dogma (Fatherhood of God, Brotherhood of Man, Non-Resistance, Vegetarianism) for that of the Church. He subscribed to a belief in the natural goodness of man which I think overwhelmingly controverted by fact, and he assigned to art a greater direct power over conduct than I believe it to possess, even when art is as rigorously censored as he demanded.

Richards is a prime example of the "nothing-but fallacy." I have great admiration for his attempt to set up a psychological theory of criticism, and so to reduce one stage, at least, of the critical act to a science. I use his system constantly, because, as I hope I have shown in the first part of this article, I am very keenly aware of the value of naturalistic systems as tools. But his procedure should have been not to argue that his "psychological" theory of value is the *only* legitimate one. He should rather have assumed the psychological theory of value as *a* legitimate basis and then have seen whether valuable results could be obtained by the method. Of course his system does not need and cannot use religious sanctions, but that does not demonstrate their lack of objective truth. I think it is clear that in order to compensate for the loss of religious sanctions he has made poetry carry a heavier burden of moral discipline than it ever, in fact, does carry.

Croce and Eastman are at poles asunder, and I shall not pause to differentiate them. The incompatibility of their systems *as a whole* with any kind of Christian orthodoxy is obvious. But though I am a professional teacher of literature and might be expected to approve of any theory which magnified the importance of poetry, I am more in accord with their fundamental positions than with those of Arnold, Tolstoi, and Richards.

I accept the conclusion that it is not of the essence of art either to reveal truth or to make men better. The artist, *qua* artist, does not show the human mind at its highest stage of development. All attempts to prove good artists to be necessarily good men are transparent sophistries. Poetry expresses mental experiences, some of which, when taken into another mind, strengthen the moral fibre, while others corrode it. Whether the moral effect is good or bad is quite immaterial so far as the *aesthetic* judgment of poetry is concerned. Milton, in *Paradise Lost*, has handled this problem of the nature of art with great subtlety. The hand of Mammon, when he fell from heaven, lost none of its cunning; he was just as good an artist in Hell as he had been in Heaven.

"Good" in criticism means two distinct things: "good as art", and "good for you". A man of saintly character who happens also to be endowed with artistic genius, will create (or at least will publish) only works of art of high seriousness, but a man of vicious character may be a very great artist. Works of art are like things which can be eaten or drunk: some of them nourish us, some are downright poisons; some, while totally unnourishing, are pleasant to the taste and do us no appreciable harm. Or works of art can be compared to the living productions of Nature: they may be useful to man, but to be useful to man is no part of the definition of their being. From the point of view of a herpetologist, a good cobra is a full-grown, healthy, typical specimen, with practicable fangs and enough poison in his sacs to kill a man. From the point of view of you and me there are no good cobras. The herpetologist's judgment corresponds to the aesthetic judgment, which is the first stage in criticism; your judgment and mine, to the moral evaluation, which is the second.

Men do not become good by refining their mental experiences. They become good by freely submitting their wills to dogmatic imperatives. For that reason poetry cannot take the place of dogma. Mr. T. S. Eliot's judgment of Arnold may also be extended to Richards:

> "Nothing in this world or the next is a substitute for anything else; and if you find that you must do without

> something, such as religious faith or philosophic belief, then you must just do without it. I can persuade myself, I find, that some of the things that I can hope to get are better worth having than some of the things I cannot get; or I may hope to alter myself so as to want different things; but I cannot persuade myself that it is the same desires that are satisfied, or that I have in effect the same thing under a different name."[24]

Science is no substitute for dogma, nor is poetry. If you cannot accept dogma for what it purports to be, you will save yourself ultimate trouble by just doing without it. I do not "believe" in the Church on prudential grounds, nor do I cultivate religion as a prop to keep my mind from sprawling. I simply believe, from participating in the Church's life, that its dogmatic pronouncements are *true*—truth supernaturally revealed in accordance with human powers. I believe that science and poetry must be given complete freedom to express the world in their own ways, but that their constructions must finally be evaluated by religion (and for me that means dogma)—not the other way about.

[24] *The Use of Poetry and the Use of Criticism*, Chap. VI. See also "Arnold and Pater" in *Selected Essays.*

V

THE CHURCH IN A DAY OF CRISIS

by

THEODORE OTTO WEDEL

Theodore Otto Wedel resigned a professorship of English and Biography in Carleton College in 1934, to become educational secretary of the Episcopal Church, with oversight of university work. He is a Bachelor of Arts of Oberlin College, a Master of Arts of Harvard and a Doctor of Philosophy of Yale. Before going to Carleton College, he taught at the University of Texas and at Yale.

APOLOGETICS is, as we all know, the defense of the Faith against its enemies. It is Christianity on a war footing. During times of peace it has often been the Cinderella among theological disciplines. Historical scholarship and dogmatic theology have frequently boasted of far greater academic triumphs. Our day, however, is not one for theological pacifism. War and war's alarms are upon us. The sanctuary has become a fortress. Christianity is now, as it was in the Roman Empire, against the world. Battling for the Christian Faith and the Christian Church is once more an adventure. Yet for this struggle, Christianity is ill prepared. For a hundred years and more, she has had to occupy herself with intramural fighting. Protestant has opposed Catholic. Orthodox has opposed modernist. Fundamentalist has faced the disillusionment of higher criticism. And all have wrestled with the avalanche of scientific thought and discovery.

Now, when at least some of those older warfares seem accomplished, but while the Christian world is still torn by inherited dissensions, the Church faces a giant enemy, compared with which former opponents appear but pygmies. She faces a world which is beginning to ignore both Catholic and Protestant, conservative and liberal, Fundamentalist and modernist. She faces a secularism which offers its own gospels of salvation—gospels which do not require belief in God or in man's repentance or in the necessity of a divine redemption, which ignore altar and Cross and prayer, which entice the populace with Utopian dreams so glamorous that even the Christian pictures of Heaven pale in comparison. As Christianity confronts this new pagan world and is girding herself for Armageddon, she must obey the law of military strategy. She must acquaint herself with the enemy.

Let us, then, look at the secularism of our time. It is a hydra-headed monster. It takes many forms and speaks with many voices. The philosophies upon which it relies range all the way from a militant atheism to a humanitarian gospel of brotherhood which, superficially considered, can with difficulty be distinguished from the Christian program. One of the simplest ways of understanding it, in fact, is to think of it as still a Christian heresy, its prophets as heirs of the Christian tradition though denying their Christian birthright. It is a gospel desirous of achieving religion's fruits without paying religion's price. It is Utopian idealism living on a stored-up capital, wasting its substance in sentimental emotions. It denies God, but believes in Man.

It was Christianity which once brought man out of pagan despair to a belief in himself as child of God and inheritor of the Kingdom of Heaven. It was Christianity which achieved the ethics of human brotherhood, of justice to the poor and downtrodden, of the dignity of labor and the joys of charity. One has merely to step back into the world of ancient

Greece and Rome to see what a social revolution was wrought by the Church. This world no longer a meaningless victim of death and corruption! Man no longer a mere creature of an hour, victim of the thievery of Time, but a being a little lower than the angels!

This Christian faith in man and in the sacramental significance of temporal creation rested upon belief in a great divine action; belief in a gift of God's grace, in an astounding story of salvation, in the death of a divine Being upon a Cross and in the payment of a tremendous price. Christianity, as long as it was aware of this foundation of its faith, found its chief and first duty in worship of the author of the great gift, in grateful penitence before the Cross, the symbol of what it had cost to make men worthy of dignity and compassion. All the Christian's achievements in personal and social goodness were motivated by a grateful response to a love which must at best leave him hopelessly in debt. At the center of his consciousness was what God had done, and was still willing to do, for those who entered the strait gate into the mystery of divine fellowship. Without that divine Grace, man was conscious of his nothingness, of his sin, of the utter precariousness of human life.

Divorce belief in the dignity of man from this gospel of God's redeeming action, emancipate man from his consciousness of dependence upon Grace, secularize the dream of God's Kingdom so as to make of it a merely temporal Utopia, and you get the secular gospels of our time. We have idealism without repentance, hope without fear of judgment, trust in human goodness without consciousness of original sin. We have humanism, a faith in Man and his power to save himself—the common denominator in all the non-Christian gospels of our day. While, in our country at least, the older Christian tradition is still tolerated and often even respected, it is beginning to be ignored. Define the goal of human striving in terms of this world, of a temporal good, however ethically lofty this may be, and the rituals of a religion dealing with things unseen begin to appear useless and a little absurd.

An analogy may serve. Time was—and not many generations since—when classical learning ruled in education. It shared with the tradition of religious culture the characteristic of being unworldly. It had no immediate utility in the market-place. The educational disciplines based upon it produced the gentleman, the man of intelligent leisure. Yet this great tradition of European education is today scarcely known. It is not fought or hated. It is simply ignored. The world has moved too fast for it. No one minds very much if a few devotees still study Greek and are still thrilled by the pages of Sophocles or Plato, provided they do not halt the procession. But such culture is plainly a luxury shouldered aside by the clamoring demands of a world of things. For this demise of classical education, its prophets and priests are, no doubt, themselves partly to blame. They were guilty of academic pride. They pursued learning in ivory towers. They refused to humble themselves to the point of practising apologetics. But no one can view the present educational scene exactly with complacence. A precious tradition has been lost. The wisdom of the ages is locked up in libraries—at a time, too, when the insight of a Plato and an Aristotle might save the world from folly and disaster.

Like all parables, mine does not perfectly apply. But is not the Christian tradition being similarly shouldered aside? Religious illiteracy is swamping us. Learning may flourish in the theological schools. Of what good is it if even the Bible is a generally unread book? Modernist Christianity may be repudiating its humanist heresies and rediscovering the romance of orthodoxy—such a thing, for example (think of Reinhold Niebuhr), as what Chesterton calls "the good news of original sin." But such heartening revolutions in the religious world are no longer front-page news. The world has outgrown them all.

Neither Fascist nor Communist nor idealistic reformer has time to waste. To wait for the philosophers to make peace with one another, to delay until the Christian liturgies have regained their hold upon a pagan people, to halt until men's hearts shall have been moved by prayer and inward revolutions (social though we grant they be), is far too slow. Hence we turn to the quick solutions of political action. We may see such action fail, as in the Prohibition experiment; but it is a failure which apparently has not taught us much. The rule of power is upon us. We can take short cuts by way of the police, by way of social law, by way at worst of class war and dictatorship. Indeed the Christian Church cannot altogether afford to oppose such appeals to power. Judgment is upon her, too. Like a Jeremiah, with Nebuchadnezzar at the gates of Jerusalem, she may see in the coming iron rule of Commissar or Storm Troops a just doom upon a misused freedom.

Edmund Burke, a hundred and fifty years ago, voiced a warning which can give us pause even today:

> "Society cannot exist unless a controlling power upon will and appetite be placed somewhere; and the less of it there is within, the more there must be without. It is ordained in the eternal constitution of things, that men of intemperate minds cannot be free."

It is quite possible, surely, that the Church will have to adjust herself to a great increase in the secular power of the State—to see in the rise of social collectivism the hand of God itself. She may recall the Hebrew prophet's words: "Assyria, the rod of my anger." Speaking for myself, I can share with my radical friends some of their realistic insight into the needs of our day for new social controls. What I cannot share is their confusing this social control with the Kingdom of God. It were as if a Babylonian captivity, necessary for the conversion of God's people, had been confused with the rebuilding of the Temple.

But the pagan world of our day is not going to read the signs of the times in the mood of a Jeremiah or of a Burke. It sees in the new age of power, not a Babylonian captivity coming as a judgment for sin, but the hope of salvation. To understand this delusion of the contemporary world, let us not underrate its attractiveness. It is indeed marvelously appealing. To confront it with the realism and otherworldly challenge of the Christian view of God and man, seems at times a hopeless venture.

Take, if you will, such a phrase (part of the stock-in-trade of contemporary sentimentalism) as "the brotherhood of man." That is an apparently obvious human ideal. It has been sung by poets from primitive times. Those who are still touched by the Christian tradition can find in Christian literature its noblest expressions. It can be extracted from the Sermon on the Mount. It looks like the gospel of Charity in I. Corinthians 13. Taken seriously, it is a gospel of revolution. It can hurl dynamite into our present industrial order.

Why not, then, take it seriously? Why not achieve it? And in achieving it, why not emancipate it from the shackles of institutional religion, take it out of the house of prayer and the communism of the altar rail into the market-place? In the final analysis, is even belief in God a necessary adjunct of it? Cannot an atheist believe in justice and equality, in peace, and in the poignant rights of the poor? Extract from the Christian tradition its apparently humanitarian ethics, and the world is prepared to bow before us. We may use force to bring in the brotherly kingdom; yes, but this is only a necessary means to an end. Why not, then, equate the gospel of salvation with the appeal to human love?

It is, in a way, a fair question. It is being asked by millions today. On the answer to it depends, quite possibly, the attitude of our time to the Christian Church.

The gospel of brotherhood, divorced fom its Christian anchorage, is only one of the forms of sentimental secularism; but it is a crucial one. Abolish the first and great commandment, or let it become a mere drop-curtain in the background. Why is not the second enough—a loving of your neighbor as yourself? Narrow this concept of who is my neighbor to racial group or economic class, and you get an even more powerful gospel, since it can ally itself to a corresponding hate, and thus bring not peace but a sword. Remove God from the cosmos and man takes on, at least at first glance, a meaning greater than he had in the Christian view. Man now is alone in a universe without a roof. There are no loving arms in a realm above the clouds. But have we not each other? We achieve comradeship and the sharing of burdens. And since a technological science has placed in our hands the tools necessary for Utopian ease, do we any longer need a God, or any of the machinery of prayer and praise addressed to the Figure of religious imagination? Make way for a practical gospel, for putting into practice at last what the Christian ethic has mouthed for too long. Let us, if indeed religion is still a thing to conjure with, have a religion without a god.

On a signboard of the Hitler Youth at Halle on the Saale one may read these words:

> "Where are the enemies of our Hitler youth? They are the religious fanatics who still today fall on their knees with wistful looks directed upward, who spend their time attending churches and praying. We, as Hitler boys, can regard only with contempt or derision

young people who still today run to their ridiculous Evangelical or Catholic clubs to give themselves up to eminently superfluous religious reveries."[1]

There you have, though in exaggerated and sketchy form perhaps, a rival religion to Christianity. It is, as I have tried to show, a Christian heresy, inconceivable in a thought-world untouched by the Christian view of man. It is a gospel of faith in man, not in God. Man, especially social man, is the source of his own salvation. It is a gospel of human pride.

As Christianity, granted that it is the Christianity of the Christian Creed and of the fellowship of the Christian mystery, confronts this secularized world, how shall it proceed? How shall it even state its case? Its very vocabulary has been forgotten, or at best is misunderstood. Even ancient words like "grace" and "sin" and "forgiveness" seem irrelevant. They imply a God. They suggest that man's first problem, yes even for the beauteous ordering of his social life, is to establish contact with his Creator. Without a belief in God, and a conviction that He is the ultimate reality, a word like "sin" loses all meaning. It implies Someone outside ourselves who cares what we do. An atheist cannot even swear.

No, the task of Christian apologetics is not an easy one today. The Church cannot condemn the newer humanist gospels on purely ethical grounds, though it may be shocked and puzzled at the racial hatred of certain Germans or at the cruelty of a Russian com-

[1] From a letter of protest sent to Chancellor Hitler by ten leaders of the confessional movement within the German Evangelical Church. Quoted in *The Living Church*, August 15, 1936, p. 153.

missar. The secularist gospel may, indeed, even be complimented for seizing upon the ideals of Christianity. The admiration for a human Jesus, so frequently found even in atheist writings, is surely right as far as it goes. Yet what a gulf divides the gospel of humanism from the historic Christian Faith! They live in different worlds of spiritual values.

Even on human grounds, we can confront the secularist gospel with two fundamental questions: first, a question regarding its goal; and second, a question regarding the means of achieving that goal.

A critic of the goal of the humanist gospel needs to point only to one fact—that such a goal is a temporal one and ignores man's hunger for eternity. Decked out in all its grandeur, with its dreams all realized, what can be its end except death? Can it, when achieved, satisfy even a fraction of the needs of man? What has it to say about

> "the proud man's contumely,
> The pangs of dispriz'd love, the law's delay,
> The insolence of office, and the spurns
> That patient merit of the unworthy takes."

All these will still be there. It might not solve even such a problem as that of the "wallflower" at a dance. No social system can equalize charm or mental talent or personal attractiveness. Yet these inequalities probably cause as much tragedy in people's lives as poverty. W. G. Peck puts this in an eloquent passage:

> "Even if it were possible to conceive the abiding establishment of a human republic, 'world-unity, with col-

laboration in the extraction, manufacture, transport and distribution of natural resources for the equal benefit of all,' apart from the tradition and realisation of a common redemption, shared grace, and an organic community of prayer and worship, what value or final spiritual relevance would reside in such an order? How would it support and refresh the heart of man, or sustain the secret dignity without which men sink from their manhood before the challenge of life and death? From any secular Utopia, where the soul meets nothing more than a worldly world, a man might turn, as Wordsworth turned from the earthly scene in his own day, ready to prefer even the dead dreams of paganism to a world where there was neither faith nor vision. Materialism and acquisitiveness, even could they be shaped into a universal collectivism, would still be materialism and acquisitiveness." W. G. Peck, *The Social Implications of the Oxford Movement*, pp. 44, 45.

Turn to the second of the questions which one must ask of the secularist gospel: granted that your goal is desirable, how can you achieve it with purely human means? Has man ever been moved much by ideals, unanchored in a faith in God?

Ideals have been cheap since the dawn of history. A child of ten could sketch a fairly adequate human Utopia. The ten commandments are not mere ideals. They are commandments of a living, righteous God, who rewards the just and the unjust. Turn the Christian gospel into nothing more than a humanitarian ideal, with the story of its central figure nothing more than an exemplarist biography, will it really for long move the hearts of men? It may simply lead to despair —as might the analogous appeal that as musician one should copy a Kreisler or a Paderewski. The Christian story has not abolished the law. But it is itself not the law, but the gospel—good news to those who have been made humble of heart by the vision and the fear of God.

The secularist gospel, with its trust in unredeemed man, must abide by that trust. It can exhort, but it cannot command, unless it appeals to the arbitrament of the sword, to G.P.U. or guillotine axe.

As G. K. Chesterton puts it, in one of his last essays:

> "I do not believe that social salvation could be achieved, or even approached, by anything like a mere improvement in social machinery, or the establishment of Bureaus for Everything. I think it happens only when there is a strong sense of duty and dignity implanted in people, not by any government or even any school, but by something which they recognize as making a secret call upon a solitary soul. I do not believe in Men like Gods; but I do believe in Men with Gods; or, preferably (such is my fastidious taste in such matters), a God." (*Avowals and Denials*, p. 128.)

It is in direct appeal once more to the realities of human experience, to the common sense of common men and women, that the hope of Christian apologetics lies. The secular gospel may fool us for a time, particularly at a time when the Church has herself at least partly played traitor to her trust; but disillusionment is sure to follow. Sooner or later, we face the ultimate questions of human life: sin and death. No amount of sentimental gilding will abolish these from human experience. Emil Brunner says in a recent essay:

"The whole of modern philosophy from Descartes on, insofar as it has not degenerated into a crass materialism and cynicism, has been a series of variations upon this one theme—the divine truth in man. The fearfulness of recent historical events has given the death blow to this faith. The problems of evil and of death, so diligently avoided by modern thought, now press upon us with their full weight. For him who can no longer disregard these two realities, the idealistic and the rationalistic thinking of the Enlightenment are forever impossible. For him there remain only two possibilities—cynicism or Christian faith. This new comprehension of human reality, this knowledge of evil, is as characteristic a starting point for the new kind of theological thinking as is the reality of God." (*Essays in Honor of William Adams Brown*, p. 173.)

Let these fundamental questions once more loom large on the horizon of consciousness, and the Christian gospel will regain a hearing, for that gospel is a gospel of redemption from evil and from death. It is a drama of salvation—the news of a great fact and of a great action, of something God has done for us by being Himself born of a Virgin and dying on a Cross.

It is precisely in the disillusionments of our time that we discover our surest hope for the revival of the Christian faith. These disillusionments are destructive fires; but in the holocaust much that is cant and sham is being devoured. The Church herself may pass through judgment and rediscover her ancient answers to the real needs of men. Above all, if only the cynical reaction is thorough enough, we shall get rid of the substitute religions of our time: our glib faith in the natural goodness of man, our hopes for a perfect world brought into being by a juggling of society's machinery, our thin trust in mere ethical culture.

The humanitarian reformers may then discover that in order to remake Society, more is needed than hopes and dreams and ideals. "Quarry the granite rock with razors"—so speaks Newman, in words to which our cynics may be led by the logic of their own analysis, "or move the vessel with a thread of silk; then may you hope with such keen and delicate instruments as human knowledge and human reason to contend against those giants, the passion and the pride of man." A this-worldly goal, even for a "good society," may be seen again, as the cynic often sees it, as not lofty enough to move man out of his selfish greed.

Gamaliel Bradford, keen observer of the souls of men, can declare:

> "I confess that I am myself perfectly, enormously egocentric, and these *ethno* considerations appeal to me very little. Insofar as the good of the race is identified with my personal comfort and well-being, I am interested in it. But my ego cries out for God simply for itself; and if it is to vanish like a dewdrop in the sun, words cannot express my utter indifference to the well-being of the race, of the world, and of the universe". (*Darwin*, p. 240.)

It is striking to note, too, how our cynical novelists are rediscovering, though by a sad inversion of values, the fact of sin and weakness in human nature. Rousseau is being disproved by his own naturalistic followers. Aldous Huxley, portrayer in his novels of a fallen human nature, states in *Proper Studies*: "The doctrine of Original Sin is, scientifically, much truer than the doctrine of natural reasonableness and virtue. . . . Primitively, and in a state of nature, human beings were not, as the eighteenth-century philosophers supposed, wise and virtuous; they were apes." In a word, "modern thought" is facing its own defeat. It ends in "sound and fury signifying nothing." Otherworldliness is its only solution. God is the only answer to the dilemma in which the cynic finds himself. Man, in order to secure peace, must go outside himself, outside even the human ideals of Society; he must find God or perish in despair.

As the Church faces this modern world, what should be its method of approach? One thing is certain. If any Christian philosophy of religion has a chance, it is one which boldly confronts our scene of intellectual chaos with an honest supernaturalism. It must proclaim once more a transcendent God—a God outside as well as inside His universe. It must strike at the root of the naturalism from which our modern heresies have sprung. The attempt to bolster up the humanitarian dream is futile. It inevitably encounters the hard facts of experience. The League of Nations is not a sufficient symbol of the Kingdom of God. Prohibition is not an answer to the cry of the human heart. The ethics of Jesus, when divorced from a gospel of salvation through the Cross, may move the listener for a day; but they, too, soon become meaningless in a world without God. Social service, the gospel of love and pity for a suffering humanity—what are they worth after all, if the fundamental questions of man's existence are not answered?

> "Admiration for 'the way of Jesus,'" says Mr. F. R. Barry in a recent book, "is not the center of Christianity, nor can it carry the weight of Christian living. There are many outside any Christian affiliation who acknowledge Christ as their example and the embodiment of their best ideals, who remain confessedly agnostic about the character or existence of God. To revere Christ's character is a precious thing, but it is not the religion of Christians. Christianity is the worship of the Father, the vision of God as revealed in Christ. For the modern mind this is the crucial difficulty. Nearly all the forces that play upon us conspire to make belief in God difficult. In the old world everyone believed in God; that is perhaps the most signal difference between ancient and modern history. The task of the earliest Christian preachers was to persuade men who believed in God to accept Christ's interpretation of Him. The task of the Church today is almost the opposite: to help people who at different levels and in various degrees believe in Christ to win conviction about God. The revival and even, it may be, the survival of Christianity in the world today depends on its success in this enterprise." *Christianity and the New World*, pp. 9-10.

A philosophy of bold supernaturalism has an appeal for the modern intellectual man or woman. There are evidences of a great hunger for God in our time. If the more moderate values of a Christian humanism are for the moment neglected, they will surely come back again. The human appeal of Jesus and the lofty ethics of the Sermon on the Mount find their rightful place in a Christian philosophy which first gives them meaning through the doctrine of the Incarnation. We are back to the days of the Early Church, when the problem of Christology was seen to be central in the Christian faith, for it is the problem of God. The problem of God, of accepting or rejecting a supernatural reality in life, haunts our disillusioned world. That world will accept, I think, either God or nothing. It can be made to respect the "foolishness of the Cross," when it has only a sneer for the petty manicuring of morals. It may scoff at the piety of our Puritan forefathers. It does not scoff at the faith of a Saint Francis.

We are rediscovering the marvel and the glory of the Christian gospel. We may, to be sure, have to pass through judgments of God before once again we hear with our ears and see with our eyes. We may, as Karl Barth suggests, have to be brought to the edge of anguish. In the lives of thousands today, this is already happening. When it does happen to a man, he is ready for the old, old story—the story of a Father who pities His children and remembers that they are but dust, Who has set us in a world of vanishing time but has redeemed us from death, Who has so loved the world (yes, this world of sin and apparently meaningless vanity of vanities) "that He gave His only-begotten Son, to the end that all who believe in Him should not perish but have everlasting life": a God who can forgive us our sins and give us the fellowship of the Holy Ghost because He has Himself suffered for us upon a Cross.

The Church, confronted with a demand for social salvation, may rediscover her own half-forgotten mission as the Kingdom and the Family of God. When all other means of social salvation have failed—the sentimentalist with his ideals and the cynic with his ruthless sword—the Church may again gather men into the brotherhood of the altar rail. That, in fact, is what we are doing when we are performing our proper task in the Church—building around the altar cells of the Kingdom of God. The motive behind that brotherhood is today, as it has been through the centuries, a response, not to mere ethical idealism nor to the law, but to God's prevenient grace. W. G. Peck declares, in an eloquent defense of the social significance of the Christian Creed:

> "When I say 'I believe in Jesus Christ, His only Son, Our Lord' I declare that I know not only what God is, but also what every man is. I know that the poorest, the vilest, has family connections with the King of Kings. If we really had got it into our heads and hearts that a human mother once bore a baby who was the eternal Son of God, we should never rest until we had made of this sin-stained and battered humanity something more worthy of such a faith. If God has become man, human personality is sacred, and we ought to flame with holy anger against all that debases it and against every interest vested in vice. No social reformer can safely set out without some doctrine of man; and there is no doctrine of man so full of revolutionary hope as this: that while we were yet sinners Christ died for us." (*The Coming of Free Catholicism*, p. 72.)

It is the very simplicity of this faith which has made it throughout the ages "unto the Jews a stumblingblock and unto the Greeks foolishness." The Gospel did not come to us in the form of a philosophy or a syllogism. To accept these might have flattered human pride. The Gospel has come to us instead in the form of a story—as simple and as astounding as a fairy tale. It is the story of God visiting man, of God manifesting His goodness in the flesh. It is utterly matter-of-fact. It took place in history. No learned doctors discovered it. We usually think of religion as man's problem—his effort to unveil the gods. In the Gospel the reverse is true. There the problem of religion is represented as God's problem—His coming to us. Christianity implies that there may no longer be a religious "problem." The other great religions of the world have tortured themselves in search for God. The greatest of them, that of Gautama the Buddha, came to the conclusion that there is no God at the end of the search. There is only the search itself. Most of the new secular gospels of our day seem like a return to such a tortured search. They, too, are engaged in man's age-long quest for salvation.

From all these, Christianity differs in its triumphant assertion that the search is ended. God has found us. He has been here. He is here now. That is why it is so breath-taking and so humiliating to human pride. Man can no longer take comfort in the heroism of exploring the unknown or of evolving endless questions. In Christianity the question has been answered. The answer must be accepted as a gift. Christianity is the announcement of a solution, not an exhortation to further search. The difficulties involved in Christian belief may not lie in the realm of intellectual doubt.

Men rebel against belief because it is so scandalously simple. We are not humble enough to accept so unimagined a solution—one which we did not achieve by all our immemorial striving.

In the simple story of the Gospel, God is a God of judgment as well as a God of mercy. He comes close to human life. Men shrink from such a visitation. It is as if our conscience, which troubles even the most audacious, suddenly comes to life and confronts us. To hide in the shelter of a law or a program or an ideal is easier than to face such a God. Hence when He came, men crucified Him.

VI

REVISIONS

by

Frank Gavin

Frank Gavin was a man of varied scholarship. Granted the primary degree from the University of Cincinnati, he perfected himself in Semitics, first at the Hebrew Union College and secondly at Harvard University, which made him Doctor of Theology in 1919. He was also a Doctor of Philosophy of Columbia University. He was Professor of History in the General Theological Seminary, New York City, and Adviser to the Episcopal Church on Ecclesiastical Relations. He was an authority on the Eastern Orthodox Communions, and wore the Cross of Miron Cristea, bestowed by the Roumanian patriarch in 1935. Dr. Gavin died while this book was in preparation.

ETYMOLOGICALLY, revision means "looking things over." In the Anglo-Catholic tradition, one of the most important characteristics for centuries has been a disposition to review the foundations of our Faith. This propensity fits in well with the general pragmatic temper of the Anglo-Saxon folk. "Looking things over" is a preliminary stage to "seeing things through". There are those of us, represented by some characters in fiction and even more in fact, whose distaste for looking things over expresses itself in overlooking things. This latter attitude of mind, however, is not to be encouraged, as it leads to little that is fruitful. It works toward too short and too easy a solution of difficulties, by way of denying their existence.

In the past, historic Christianity has not been without those who have been endowed with the capacity to overlook too much. In the early days of the Church, when after small beginnings, at last hoards of heathen clamored at the Church's doors for admission into her fellowship, the stunned surprise of Christians at the change in circumstances made the welcome they extended all too easy. Too much was overlooked. Thence arose innumerable heresies and schisms. In the expansive hospitality of a Church suddenly grown popular and welcomed in powerful quarters, a disposition not to scrutinize accompanied the outstretched hand.

Early Christianity would have been spared much had it verbally transposed the action from "overlooking things" to "looking things over". For example, the theological contrabrand brought in by Eastern converts constituted a problem of such magnitude that in the second century the Docetists and other types of pragmatic Dualists offered great hindrances to the unity, both in faith and practice, of the early Catholic Church. Throughout her history, the Church's human agents have been too guilty of lack of insight. At so late a date as the Reformation, to name only one instance, the easily accepted assumption on the Catholic side as to the verbal inerrancy and infallibility of every word of Holy Scripture is evidence of this lack of penetration. Had the corporate mind of the Church been alert to the steady and properly continuous task of revision, many of these controversies might have been avoided.

In such matters, goodwill is not enough. Along with goodwill must stand intelligence, understanding, and that kind of intuitive awareness which senses what is not expressed and feels that which is not articulate. It is futile to expect a religion that addresses itself to the whole of a man, not to reckon with intellectual expression. Again and again, the easy-going quasi-sentimentality of the corporate body of Christians has let the case for Christianity go by default, merely for lack of capacity and lack of interest to reinterpret and restate.

Vision, prevision, and revision are all closely associated with each other. From the human point of view, at the outset of the spiritual pilgrimage especially, the Vision of God is all-important. Inevitably awareness of what God is like, of what He says, and of what He wills finds its expression in human terms. This articulate expression in turn becomes a kind of chart of direction, as it were, a diagrammatic scheme of exploration for the soul's journeyings in this world.

Vision leads to prevision. What we know has been, helps condition our expectations of what is to be. What we have come to learn of the past by our incorporation into the great stream of tradition by which this past becomes our past, serves among other purposes this: it enables us to have some prevision of the future. In both respects, however, the steady task of looking over again that which has been given, experienced, expressed, and taught is incumbent upon each generation of Christians. Revision is commanded by a spiritual categorical imperative.

In the pages that follow I invite attention to the consideration of some six topics within the tradition of Christianity commonly called Catholic: Sin, Salvation, the Saviour, Sacraments, Sanctity, and Society.

I. Sin

To the modern world the conception of Sin is completely outmoded. As is the case with the conception of virtue, so that of Sin has come to lack savor and validity. The meaningfulness of the word has to a large degree departed. It has been invested with connotations so far removed from the original ideas that what is conceived of in common parlance is very wide of the original mark.

We of the West have been over-ridden for centuries by a sheerly legalistic conception of Sin and transgression. Whatever truth there be in this way of looking at things, the fact remains that the truth so expressed owes its chief survival value to its practical simplicity. It is vastly more easy to be able to list one's faults and sins in black and white, in accordance with a prearranged catalogue, than to come to terms with the reality of which such expressions and descriptions are but symbols. Just insofar as man is a legal animal and entity this juridic conception of sin meets the facts—but no further. In these days in which we live, we have in part recovered something of the early Christian attitude toward Society as an organic whole in which the units are individuals not in a complete sense but only relatively. Were we to shift the accent of interest and emphasis from the forensic to the biological, we should be nearer the truth.

Sin is "transgression of the law." What is the normative law for us, and whence is its authority? So long as men conceived of the universe as ruled over by an Oriental potentate whose will was the law and whose word was its expression, it was entirely consonant and congenial to think of sin in terms of a transgression of the law, either voluntary or involuntary. That this conception is both as congenial, nay as necessary, to many people today as it has been in the past, is without question. That it is ultimately satisfactory is, on the other hand, very doubtful.

When St. Augustine discussed the elements of Sin, his acute perception of the actual psychological factors led him to write of it: "Through blindness man fails to see, or through weakness man fails to accomplish that which he ought to do". The great Father of the West thus states two elements–unawareness, and incapacity–which have to do with sinfulness. Not unlike him, St. Clement of Alexandria had long before thought through certain factors: "Sinning arises from being unable to determine what ought to be done, or being unable to do it". We are then led on, by one of the great Fathers of the East and by the greatest representative of the West, to a consideration of these two all-important factors: lack of vision and lack of power.

Implicit in the former element is, of necessity, ignorance. Knowledge of a sort may be present; but this knowledge is not realization. Vision there may be, but not full insight. What is perceived is a relatively small area of the whole scope of the soul's span of encompassment. Sensitiveness and responsiveness to the ideal is one of the most important elements of virtue. The life of virtue, in short, consists in progressive enlightenment, in a steady growth of perception and awareness. This perception would itself be truly demoralizing, were it to exist alone. What is needed is effective implementation, to correspond and cooperate with that which is being seen. Hence, spiritual power as well as insight is necessary for the virtuous life, as the lack of both constitutes the essence of sinfulness in action.

It is to be noted that both these characteristics—lack of awareness and lack of power—belong to the youthful state of life. To be unaware and also to be weak, would be to St. Clement, as to St. Augustine, the constituent elements of sinfulness. So far as I know, few of the Fathers saw what were the implications involved. Growth in awareness, like physical and mental growth, is part of a process. Initiation and sustenance of this progress appear in the form of acts, of which the initial one is by the Grace of God in cooperation with the will of man. Little stress was laid upon the progressive and dynamic quality of growth and vitality in the definition of Sin most commonly current in the early Catholic tradition.

There have not been lacking those, however, who fastened upon a different aspect of the whole problem. Awareness and sensitiveness deal with a relationship between means and ends, and so St. Athanasius defines Sin as "mistaking the means for the end". This definition carries our consideration several steps further. We have the picture of a person who is growingly sensitive, whose horizon is steadily expanding. Within that horizon are the elements of choice and action, arranged in a kind of hierarchy, as if in a complete network of interrelationships.

St. Athanasius saw the difference between a sinner and a saint in the increasing awareness on the part of the latter of intrinsic relationships between the vision of the soul and the business of living. He was not blind to the fact that, for the effective transaction of life, again and again it is necessary to accept a necessary means almost as if it were an end in itself, though to do so on any other principle than that of expediency would appear to be a complete denial of ultimate values. Distortion of outlook and a proclivity to hasty action are characteristic of the partly aware person who is as yet not completely equipped with the necessary capacity for the fully virtuous life.

Confounding means with ends, due to short-sightedness and lack of awareness, is another way of saying that the sinfulness of a sinful act comes about through the non-recognition of relationships. There are not lacking those in the early Christian tradition who saw this point. For example, Tatian actually defines Sin in terms of the non-recognition of limitations, which is another way of saying the repudiation of fixed relationships. Throughout the history of Christianity, the central dogma of the Incarnation is the sublime and eternal recognition of limitation, as a necessary step toward transcending it. The sinfulness of Sin would thus consist in the inability to see things whole, and clearly. St. Clement would make a "mistake" to be really a "sin contrary to calculation". Underlying this whole type of early Christian thinking, which is really fresh and modern, is the sense that Sin belongs inevitably to an undeveloped stage of our being.

II. Salvation

Perhaps more than any other term in the current Christian vocabulary, the word "Salvation" has come to be divested of all persuasive power and attractiveness. For the past several generations, Salvation commonly meant being saved from the pains of damnation and hell. Religion was frequently urged, in practical apologetics, as a divinely provided device to enable the believer to escape the penalties of his own actions, by a kind of spiritual magic wrought by God. Salvation generally meant something negative. It was almost always preached, too, as something individualistic; and it is extremely difficult not to see in this view of salvation a self-centered and selfish appeal.

When we turn to the pages of the New Testament or the writings of the Church Fathers, it is easy to perceive how far the common acceptance of the term has drifted from what Our Lord taught and what the Church at her best has believed. Salvation really means, of course, fulness of life. Throughout the writings of the Fathers, the incessant dwelling upon "renovation" and the reiterated emphasis upon new vitality flowing from Christ bear testimony, by way of commentary, to the Johannine summary of the dominical teaching given in St. John x.10. It is lamentable that this quality in the conception of Salvation is not brought more to the fore today. The Catholic Faith has always thought of Salvation dynamically rather than statically, and positively rather than negatively.

Beneath the whole conception of man's Salvation are found two poles of Christian thinking about man: the one, the high dignity of man's estate as son of God; the other, the doctrine of the Fall. At this point it may not be without value to remember to what an extraordinary extent the full-orbed Christian tradition has presented and retained this paradox, a central factor in man's experience of life. Man is told that he is both a son of God whose high dignity is unique in the order of creaturedom and, in the same breath, that he has failed to manifest effective sonship. It is as if to say that the life-stream pulsing through the heart of God to humanity is blocked and frustrated by refusal to give it full play in the hearts of men. In this sense, the barrier to effective sonship is the refusal to keep on growing in the direction of the family type that God has given us by creation and redemption.

The deadly paralysis that precludes growth is offset by the new life which God gives in His Son. This New Life, so often testified to in all the earliest Christian writings, constitutes the heart of the gospel message of Salvation. There must obviously be stages in the process. To be saved *for* the new life means to be saved *from* the old life. What is bad about the latter is that it is incomplete life, so incomplete and partial as to be reckoned death rather than life. The inculcation, so often taught by St. Paul, of ascetic practice, is for the purpose of a higher sensitiveness and the consequent generation of a deeper and growing awareness of spiritual values. Inasmuch as the Christian religion postulates that human nature has the capacity for almost infinite growth, the conception of Salvation must of necessity be progressive and dynamic rather than static. The true and full Christian tradition can never stop short in the cultivation of negative virtues, nor rest content at any stage of the unfolding life which is Salvation. The infinite yearnings of the human soul bespeak a capacity and need which only God Himself can satisfy.

Perhaps the best place to find a parallel in early Christianity to the comparison here being advanced both of Sin and Salvation, is in the idea of the "true Gnostic" as expounded by St. Clement. Were the ideal character there described that of a spiritually mature personality, no harm would be done to the thinking and a step taken toward its better interpretation. For perspective to St. Clement meant precisely the encompassment of fulness of vision and maturation, the high use of intelligent insight and the transcending of the impulses of emotion. St. Clement also goes so far as to say that for him faith has passed into knowledge. The statement needs safeguarding, as he well knew. The conception of the imperfect person, not yet fully grown-up, and that of the ideal man of spiritual insight and virtuous self-discipline, shed light on the relationship between the fact of Sin and the need of Salvation. Fulness of life, then, ever growing, ever more realized, ever more profoundly deepened—is Salvation.

III. The Saviour

Salvation would mean little to the Christian apart from *the Saviour*. He it is who is the Bringer of Life to mankind. It is through contact with Him, in all the various ways in which the Word has manifested Himself in history, that new life comes to man. He spake by the prophets; but also He has spoken, and still speaks, through the inspired men of all times and all places. The Word spake before the Incarnation, though His complete self-utterance was when "The Word became Flesh and dwelt among us". In other words, there are many old testaments and many John Baptists who pointed the way to Christ. The process, which began with the Annunciation, is still fulfilling itself in human history; the saving work is still going on.

The Saviour's life and example brought, explicitly, an entirely novel element into God's relation to His universe. Insofar as the innovatory work wrought at the Incarnation took place in Time and Space, it had about it a once-for-all quality that makes repetition impossible. Insofar as it was the Infinite One who translated Himself into the terms of the temporal and creaturely, all that He did and was partakes of an infinite quality. And so, while in one sense the Incarnation is a fact of the past, in another it is an ever-present and continuous event.

The saving work of Christ consisted, in part, of the Atonement. When the word "Atonement" is used, one is immediately sensible of the countless arenas of debate and of theological controversy that have taken place in regard to it. The fundamental conception of the Atonement is extremely simple: "God was in Christ reconciling the world unto Himself".[1] To St. Athanasius, the whole life of Our Lord was Atonement. There are not lacking others of the earliest tradition of Christianity, notably St. Irenaeus, who

[1] II Corinthians 5:19.

thought of Our Lord as summing up in Himself the whole of past and present humanity, in order that He might recapitulate what had been and, as it were, "capitulate" that which humanity was yet to be. For the most part, the earlier Fathers (and especially the Greeks) regarded the Crucifixion as only an event, though an important event, in the whole process of the Atonement. For the most part, in the West, attention was directed again and again, too exclusively, to Calvary.

What was it that Our Lord did upon Calvary to achieve the Atonement? First of all, He made, as it were, a public apology to God for the sin of man. Secondly, He offered a complete obedience to the Will of God which, by virtue of what He was as both God and man, erased the disobedience of the wayward and stubborn will of recalcitrant humanity. Thirdly, He took upon Himself, in an exemplary fashion, the pains and suffering that inevitably result, the ills produced in humanity, by its own short-sighted and selfish actions. Fourthly, He showed the high dignity of human capacity. His Incarnation and all His actions, before and at and after Calvary, were no less a revelation of what man would be, and really was, than of the nature of God.

IV. Sacraments

In the sixteenth century, Western Christendom was split on what was fundamentally the basic attitude toward the material universe and human nature. This is obvious when one investigates what the Sacraments mean to the Churches of the West. It is hard for the western-born Protestant not to see in the Catholic view of the Sacraments something which smacks both of magical and mechanical legerdemain. All too often, the Catholic of the West has given the impression that the sacramental life of the Church is a kind of automatic machine, which mankind can manipulate to achieve different effects in the realm of the spirit. There have not been lacking those of the past several centuries who in the West have spoken of sacramental grace in terms which lend themselves to such misinterpretation. The graciousness of God with reference to man is, for the Protestant, primarily administered in the great Sacrament of Preaching. It is the ministry of the Word which to him is all-important. The ministry of the Sacraments (or, as he prefers to call them, "ordinances") has a subsidiary place. In making such a statement I am aware that this is not true in all cases; but on the whole it represents a characteristic element in Protestant belief and practice, especially when the Protestant attitude is compared with the iterated emphasis on sacramentalism to be found in western Catholicism.

A revision of sacramental terminology is much needed today. So much stress has been put upon the Sacraments that almost it might appear that God Himself were being neglected in a concentration upon the divinely appointed means of receiving the Grace He has bestowed. Revision would mean first of all the correction of perspective and the re-evaluation of the high importance of sacramental belief and practice, in relationship to the whole nexus of doctrine and action commonly called Catholic. Divergencies between the Protestant and Catholic attitudes are manifold. In theory, the Catholic is as devoted to the Ministry of the Word as to that of the Sacraments; in practice the former is perhaps neglected in an overemphasized devotion to the latter.

It surely should be unnecessary to note that the stringent Catholic definition of the Sacraments precludes any possible notion that they are magical or mechanical in operation; but it is precisely at this point that divergent convictions make themselves manifest. The Protestant has great difficulty in accepting this statement as true. The Catholic all too often overlooks the high importance of making the non-magic of the Sacraments articulately clear. Such mutual and unnecessary misunderstandings generate mutual distrust, where they do not beget overt hostility.

What the Catholic means by the whole sacramental outlook depends ultimately upon certain premises in his thinking, and immediately upon explicit convictions. To the former category belongs a view of the universe, held by all Catholics, in which matter and spirit are regarded not as enemies but as allies, in which each complements the other and both fulfill the purpose of the one God who created them both. Also, the Catholic thinks of human nature in a fashion at once optimistic and realistic. In the debates at Trent, one thing was clearly manifest: the Protestants were convinced that a good God could not leave the essential ministry of His Grace to the agency of fallible man, while the Catholics were equally convinced that He not only could but had been logically bound to do nothing else than that.

Another popular Protestant misconception is that the Catholic believer in sacramentalism disbelieves in any means of grace other than the Sacraments. It would be gratuitous to attempt any kind of documentation to prove that this is untrue. The same God of grace is the minister of all its dispensation, both through and outside the Sacraments. Catholics do not always make this clear. The unfortunate misconception, again, that the Sacraments convey a spiritual commodity, or are surcharged with a kind of intrinsic energy, or in an impersonal fashion release a source of power, has, as was suggested, a good deal to justify its existence, if all one has to go on is the *popular* terminology of too many western Catholic writers.

The Sacraments are opportunities, occasions rather than transactions of Divine Grace. How vastly important the distinction is, may appear when one contrasts a highly mechanical, even if not magical, view of the Sacraments, with a more carefully phrased doctrine. God never works with man in such a fashion as to vitiate the freedom of the human will. He never so deals with us that, as it were, a lower order in the hierarchy of existence becomes the vehicle of the higher. The Catholic thinks of the physical and material as not only conjoined with the spiritual, but almost as equal to the spiritual (if equality can be postulated when the elements under discussion are as diverse as they appear to be).

No, there is nothing mechanical or magical about the Sacraments. God's Grace, even in the Sacraments, is in no sense coercive, nor is its operation invariably certain of securing good results in the case of any given believer. Man's own cooperative attitude is as much of importance in the partnership by which God has dignified man's status with Him, as is God's own part in the relationship. The transformation of values which comes about through the application of the sacramental principle has its roots in the Mystery of the Trinity and the awful solemnity of the Incarnation. The Sacraments minister the means of salvation by furnishing the occasion and the opportunity whereby the free will of mankind may lay hold on Him Who is eternal.

V. Sanctity

Sanctity, as commonly conceived, is no more palatable to this age in which we live than are some of the other conceptions that have been touched upon. In common parlance, sanctity has been suffused with the same quality of connotations that other words have unfortunately acquired–for example, "piety" and "sanctimoniousness". As the man in the street understands these words, all three convey an impression of aloofness, smugness, complacency, and spiritual superiority.

There has been much occasion given, in the working

out in practice of Catholic tradition, for this state of affairs. All too often the Christian life has been talked of by the Catholic as a sort of collector's paradise in which one set himself earnestly to "acquire virtues". The same type of thinking is evinced by those whose great preoccupation is with collecting rare editions, Chinese porcelain, stamps, or some other rarity that gives joy, or at least satisfaction, to the possessor. A subtle flavor of acquisitiveness has marked the inculcation of piety in too many quarters in western Christendom. All too often, the ideal as portrayed in books of devotion is far from virile or robust. It is frequently negative instead of positive, and a strong virus of both imported and inherent Puritanism has been conspicuous in Catholic devotions ever since the Reformation. We must revise our notions as to what constitutes Catholic sanctity.

The holiness and example of the shrewd "Gnostic" in St. Clement's writings, is not of this quality. Nor for that matter was it so with St. Athanasius, whose opponents denounced him as domineering and aggressive. The vigor of polemic and denunciation on the part of such men as St. John Chrysostom, St. Hilary of Poitiers and St. Jerome, and the strong passion of the early Religious, surely manifested no signs of a negative attitude. On the contrary, such men displayed vigor and almost violence in the pursuit of the good.

Sanctity is really the attribute of those who are single-minded in following the Will of God, to which they give themselves entirely and without reserve, by way not of passive acceptance but of active cooperation. Sanctity is not all of one type. There are mystical and practical saints. There are saints intellectual and saints executive. There are administrative saints and poetical saints. The rich variegation and flowering of the individual within the corporate Body of Christ, is one of the true notes of Sanctity. The saint, like St. Paul, never counts himself to have attained, but presses on. There is in him no serenity of satisfaction, no complacency in conquests achieved. There is, to be sure, an inner peace; but it is a peace like that on the bridge of a battleship in the midst of battle.

The saint is one who has transformed the futility of frustration into fruitfulness, by an ever-progressive adjustment of himself to the sublime realities. The saint is distinguished by his capacity to transform apparent defeat into virtue, and accepted limitations into the very means of an extended power and effectiveness. The saint seeks not the resolution of conflict, nor escape from strains and tensions. His achievements, he would say, are the work of God's grace, and it is God's will which is the sole thing that lies before him. We have done wrong in translating "katharoi kardia" in the Beatitude as "pure in heart". It actually means single-minded or single-purposed. The saint is conspicuously the person of the "integrated life". All that he is and does is enucleated about God's Will. His blessing is that "he shall see God".

The savor of Sanctity is irresistible to those who are sensitive and aware. The sheer holiness of a good man or woman makes its own appeal, and is its own verification. Moreover, both in essence and in relationship,

Sanctity is contagious. Nothing challenges blind obstinacy more, or the wilful waywardness of voluntary ignorance, as does sheer Sanctity. While difficulties and obstacles inevitably surround the pathway on which the saint walks, his sense of the proportion of things never deserts him.

This sense of proportion is closely akin to a sense of humor—instance the famous story of St. Teresa who, when murmuring at being driven forth on a dark and rainy night from one of the convents she had tried to reform, was assured by Our Lord that His friends always "had the hard path", to Whom St. Teresa made answer: "Your Majesty, that is the reason that you have so few friends."

The sense of proportion is an awareness of relationships, and is closely akin to that quality described as humility. There is no tinge of anything approximating Uriah Heep in the humility of the saint. Deep penitence there is, but it is dynamic; self-abnegation too, but it is shown in an unboasting and unconscious dignity. The recovery of the inescapable charm of holiness and sanctity is part of the task today, as well in Christian apologetics as in the preaching and practice of the Catholic life in general.

VI. Society

Not only is man primarily a social animal by nature, but also in the supernatural life as well his corporate and social needs are given the superior place. Catholicism cannot be practiced in private, since the Church (that living organism on earth whose Head is in Heaven), while having nothing, yet possesses all things. The sanctification and transformation of Society proceed fundamentally, for the Catholic, from the dogmas of traditional Christendom. God, who is Himself a Society of Three Persons, is yet Himself one Unity. In His very being there is Trinity in Unity. He by His creative and redemptive work has once and for all shown us both the essential solidarity of the human race and the corporate quality of Christianity.

When we view Society as it now exists in our industrialized civilization, long since become secularized because of political and economic pressure, there can hardly fail to be deep sympathy for the indictment of the political order that St. Gregory VII so vigorously pronounced in his famous letter to Hermann of Metz. Society apart from God is a sacrilege. Social, political and economic organization without reference to His Will for man; the subordination of human beings to be used as pawns by the few who make them means for their own peculiar ends; the deadly crushing of personality and the complete callousness to any principle of man's inherent rights both as an individual and as a member of Society:—all these are patently parts of the secularism in which we are living today.

The Catholic Faith is a religion that demands all or nothing. Its organic quality is based upon dogma. There is true demandingness. *The Christian life allows for no compromise with the princes of this world.* Diluted Christianity is a good deal like diluted virtue, so weak an antiseptic solution that it can dilute even the dominical demands. *The full strength of the Faith* will be needed if Society is to be redeemed.

VII

The permanent and unchanging in that Faith once for all delivered to the Saints, if it is to remain permanent and unchanging, must continually express itself in new statement. It was St. Clement who said: "If the assertions made by us appear to . . . be different from the Lord's Scriptures, let it be known that it is from that source that they have taken breath and life; and taking their rise from them, they profess to *adduce the sense only, not the words*" (*Stromateis* VII.1).

The same thought can be found in Vincent of Lerin's *Commonitory*:

> " 'Keep that which is committed to thy trust' (1 Tim. vii. 20). What is it which is 'committed to thy trust'? It is that which is *committed* to thee, not that which thou hast found out thyself; that which thou hast received, not that which thou hast thought out for thyself; a matter not of the exercise of thy talents but of teaching, not of private possession but of public tradition; a matter that has been brought down to thee, not one which has come forth from thee—in which thou thyself art not author but guardian, not the originator but the follower, not the leader but the led. . . . The same things which thou hast learned, these teach, so that *when thou sayest them in a new fashion thou do not say new things*. But perhaps someone may say 'Is there in the Church of Christ no development of religion to be had?' Yes, there is, obviously, and very great it is too; . . . but it must be such that, while

there is a development in that Faith, there is no change in its essence" (22.23).

The representation of the old Faith may make it seem new; but the test of its integrity comes about through a perennial vitality. It is its continuous life that matters.

VII

TO RELIGION THROUGH BEAUTY

by

Ralph Adams Cram

Ralph Adams Cram is an artist and a philosopher. As senior member of the firm of Cram and Ferguson, he has been associated with the rebuilding of West Point and many universities and colleges, including Princeton, Williams and Sweetbriar. Hundreds of churches in America are the work of his firm, chief among them the Cathedral of St. John the Divine in New York. He is the author of twenty books, some on architecture and other arts, others on politics and sociology. He is the holder of doctorates from Princeton, Yale, Williams and Notre Dame, and a member of many learned societies in the United States and England.

WHEN the sub-man of the Old Stone Age became man in a true and historical sense (less by slow process of evolution than by an almost catastrophic transformation), two new qualities signalized that truly epoch-making event, and gave to the new creation a unique status. He, this new creature, in whom had been implanted an immortal soul, in earnest of his new estate sought to create for himself religion, and also to compass the achievement, by the work of his own hands, of beauty. Since that significant moment, except for one short period—short as time is counted by human scale—beauty and religion have never been put asunder.

Paleolithic proto-man (I put to one side the Cro-Magnon mystery which has not yet been solved but which, antecedent to the Paleolithic, was yet not its progenitor but something quite other) was kin to the beasts of his worldly environment. Like them he was conditioned by the several physical needs and impulses that continue to control animal lives. When the immortal soul was smitten into the animal frame, man became a person; he became conscious of powers outside himself, of sanctions other than those imposed by physical necessity, of creative ability above that implied in the chipping of flint tools. Out of imagination, which had come with his new estate as man, he fashioned for himself religions of one sort and another, and he also felt suddenly the need and the impulse to create some sort of beauty through his own handiwork. The oldest things we have of the works of man give evidence of his religious promptings, and the artifacts he has left show his first efforts at ornament and the achievement of beauty.

His religion dealt with that which was *outside* himself, higher than himself. The beauty he wrought was also something beyond himself; a wonder, in some sense a mystery. It was the best thing he could do; and therefore he was impelled to associate it with that other mystery, his religion, and to give it, sometimes in honor, sometimes in sacrifice, to the gods he worshipped.

In the fourth millennium before Christ, in Memphis and its necropolis of Sakkarah, man-made beauty first appears. It is beauty of as high an order as that which was achieved in Greece three thousand years later. Apparently it came by some process of parthenogenesis, for behind is nothing but the crude dolmens and the rough artifacts of the Neolithic race. Religion came contemporaneously with this art. Suddenly there seems to have come to man a consciousness of immortality, belief in a life after death. The pyramids, from Medum and Sakkarah to those of Gizeh, were sepulchral monuments, but when they were built to guard the bodies of dead Kings, each had its great temple of worship attached to it. The temples are gone, but the pyramids still stand.

From this moment, which may well be called the

beginning of human history—the beginning of time so far as man is concerned—religion has inspired art and art has served religion—until a few centuries ago, when, for the first time in six thousand years, the golden cord began to be snapped and the relationship forgotten. Through all those ages what was engendered by the religious impulse was at once transmitted to artistic handling of secular things. The art that showed itself in all the works of man, from the kitchen and its utensils to the palace and its furnishings—the beauty that man created through a score of arts, in a hundred styles and modes, over six thousand years of time and in the four quarters of the globe, was at once the offspring of a religious prompting and valid evidence of the integrity and nobility of man as a new creature, evidence of his kinship with the supra-human forces of the cosmos and of his dominion over all other forms of created life.

There is no need to catalogue the works of concrete beauty that the human race has produced since art appeared on the banks of the Nile. Perhaps one one-hundred-thousandth part still remains after time and ignorance, war and greed, savagery and hatred have played their part in wide destruction; but that little is enough to prove that in the arts, if anywhere, man shows the result of the touch of the finger of God. We, in our own day, are inordinately proud of electrical refrigerators and submarines, talking movies and turbine generators, sanitary plumbing and aeroplanes; but the mutilated shards of the beauty that man has made for himself are a greater gauge of his humanity.

The diorite statue of Zoser, the *Venus of Milo* and the *Beau Dieu* of Amiens; the Parthenon of Athens, *Hagia Sophia* in Constantinople and Bourges Cathedral; Giotto's frescoes in Padua, da Vinci's *Last Supper*, El Greco's *Burial of Count Orgaz*; a Bach concerto; a Beethoven symphony, a Wagner opera; Homer's *Odyssey*, *The Divine Comedy*, Shakespeare's *Tempest* —these are enduring evidences of the creative power of man.

When a Neolithic potter scratched geometrical devices on his clay bowl, he started something that ended up with the Victory of Samothrace, Memling's *Adoration of the Virgin*, the Capella Palatine of Palermo. In these things man has attained his majority; after them have been only multiplication and differentiation. The patterns on the clay bowl turned a merely useful utensil into a work of art. The potter did not know this. He was only acting under the new impulse that came to him with his manhood. He and his successors for thousands of years did things beautifully not because they were "artists" (that *genus* has never been differentiated from the common run of men except when some phase of culture was in decline) but because they liked what they did to look that way and because it seemed the right thing to do. If it was very good, it acquired *value* in his eyes and so he felt impelled to bury it with his dead or to offer it at some sanctuary of the gods. From this to the tentative fashioning of "idols", symbolical presentments of a dimly apprehended divinity, was an inevitable step.

Thus with passage of time came the supreme sculptures of Egypt, Greece, the Middle Ages, the Early Renaissance, China, Japan.

Beauty became both sacrifice and creative expression. Imagination, transcending experience, made art the vehicle of the Ideal; so to speak, its sacramental expression, "the outward and visible sign of an inward and spiritual grace." Religion became a thing ocularly to be manifested by man to man. And so it became something more than simple expression. It acquired and exerted dynamic force. Religion that had once been only an emotion, an aspiration,—at the worst a superstition—now became a visible reality; it acquired power. Besides the few—mystics, philosophers, saints—who could lay hold of the abstract Ideal and come in immediate relationship with Deity, there were also the multitudes who "had to be shown." Every religion that has spread and maintained itself has done so quite as much through the concrete beauty of its artistic expression—its architecture, sculpture, painting, poetry, music, ritual—as through the exhortations of prophets, the preaching of evangelists, even the lives of holy men and women.

Beauty is not truth, truth beauty, as has sometimes been said; but beauty is for the people an infallible test of truth, whether in art, in conduct, philosophy or religion. The ugly thing, man knows to be untrue.

In the beginning the pathway to art was through religion. Is a reversal now possible? Through art may we find a way back to religion?

I use the words, "art" and "beauty", as synonymous terms, for so they were implicitly held until a generation ago. Of course the quality and the degree of beauty achieved from time to time in the arts varied greatly, but it was always something ardently sought for. Even when beauty was comparatively of a low order, as during a part of the Dark Ages, or during the reign of the English Elizabeth (except in literature), or during the Counter-Reformation in Italy, or in England and America under the Puritans, there was at least an honest effort at the accomplishment of a certain sort of beauty. It is only in the last few years that, for some obscure reason, a small but vocal group of human beings has sought to reconcile art with ugliness. Of late the Congo fetish, Epsteinian sculpture, Dalistic surrealism, Corbussierian architecture and instrumental cacophany, have been fantastically exalted as "art". This pathological episode need not detain us, for it can claim no more permanency than the earlier (and slightly more plausible) flairs for *art nouveau* and the "Mission style" and *clôche* hats. I speak of it here, in passing, simply because it shows how far it is possible to go when the cord of tradition is broken, standards of value are denied or reversed, and anarchy exalted in place of order. Through this sort of thing there is, of course, no line of approach to religion. If a way to religion is to be found it must be through arts that seek beauty as their goal.

From the outbreak of the Protestant revolution, the old kinship between beauty and religion was deprecated and often forgotten. Not only was there, amongst the reformers and their adherents, a definite hatred of beauty and a determination to destroy it when found; there was also a conscientious elimination of everything of the sort from the formularies, services and structures that applied to their new religion. In this these protagonists of religious rebellion showed great perspicacity, for instinctively they realized the significance and the power of persuasion to the older, tested religious ways inherent in the man-made but God-inspired beauty against which they had set their hands. Doctor Luther was less logical than some of the others; he liked the old things even when he denied what they stood for. But the more shrewd counsels of Doctor Calvin and Doctor Knox prevailed, first in the English-speaking lands and a little later in Germany and Holland, and at last what had become un-significant beauties disappeared largely from Lutheranism too.

It would be difficult to establish a greater antithesis than that between a pre-Reformation church—any one in any land—and the conventicles that succeeded. In Europe and the British Isles new churches were not needed. Indeed, a good many of those that were left were destroyed as useless. In those countries all that needed to be done was to break up the altars, shrines and tombs, to smash the stained-glass windows, whitewash the painted walls, mutilate the statues and tear down a nave here, a choir or transepts there. Into the empty and desecrated shell was introduced a new type of service, barren of beauty, and the thing was done.

In the United States the situation was quite different. Here there was no Catholic art to destroy, churches (or "meeting houses") had to be built. Even if "divine worship" now consisted only in the reading of passages from the Scriptures, some metrical psalms, extemporaneous prayers and sermons that often ran to two hours in length, a place had to be provided for these exercises. The brick masons, carpenters and shipwrights did the best they could, according to their lights. Frequently they did pretty well, especially when they were working for aristocratic and "reactionary" Church of England parishes; but they had to be content with the bare fabric. No art except that of building could be used. The shell might have good proportions, simplicity of form and honesty of construction; but within, the edifice was as cold and dreary as the services.

Tradition of sorts still lingered, to be sure, and this first "religious architecture" in America was certainly as good as, sometimes better than, what was being produced in the mother country. When, however, early in the last century, that tradition died of starvation and neglect, as it always will in time under such circumstances, the end even of good church architecture came swiftly. For fifty years, with a very few exceptions, the churches built in America, together with the few products of religious arts other than architecture, were without doubt the most barbarous, uncouth and reprehensible structures ever erected by man since Imhotep built his temples at Sakkarah.

Simultaneously, though for quite different reasons and under a different compulsion, the Old Faith had been keeping step, artistically, with the new. The Renaissance froze even Catholic art into immobility, and that art began to rot into aesthetic corruption. The religious arts, once so supreme, including ritual and ceremonial, pursued a career of progressive vulgarizing and deterioration. Catholic art of every kind in America matched and sometimes exceeded Protestant art in point of flatulence and ineptitude. The severance between religion and beauty had been accomplished.

This unprecedented break between religion and beauty had a good deal to do with that waning interest in religion itself which has resulted in a state of things where less than half the people in the United States have even formal affiliation with any religious organization. It was a case of interaction. The "age of reason and enlightenment" had resulted in undermining the normal faith in spiritual realities, and in persuading man that there were no valid sanctions beyond those he determined for himself by the simple process of personal ratiocination. At the same time Protestantism, with its derivative materialistic rationalism, was divesting religion of its essential elements of mystery and wonder, and worship of its equally essential elements of beauty. Under this powerful combination of destructive influences, it is not to be wondered at that, of the once faithful, many have fallen away, or that youth came to be bored by ineptitudes and offended by artistic sterility and vacuous ugliness.

In spite of certain contemporary phenomena, human beings still retain a normal hunger for beauty. Modern civilization is working overtime to atrophy this, and has achieved a good measure of success; but there is always a revulsion against a thing that is carried too far. The very absurdities of artistic "modernism" are bringing about a wholesome reaction. A really good work of architecture, or of any other art, gains instinctive and enthusiastic recognition, while the degenerate aberrations begin to elicit laughter and disgust outside the narrow circle of their protagonists and commercial purveyors. One proof of this is the almost unbelievable transformation of ecclesiastical architecture, both Catholic and Protestant, that has taken place in the United States during the last fifty years. Against this phenomenal recovery, or restoration, the occasional aberrations of the "functionalists" are as impotent as they are minor in number and magnitude.

Man is, by instinct, not only a lover of beauty, he is also by nature a "ritualist"; that is to say, he does, when left alone, desire form and ceremony, if significant. People may not realize it clearly, but they do believe in symbol—also if significant. Under Protestantism the symbol was first emptied of meaning and then, very naturally, thrown away. If this instinctive craving for ceremonial is denied to man in religion, where it preëminently belongs, he takes it on for himself in secular fields; elaborates ritual in secret societies, in the fashion of his dress, in the details of social custom. He also, in desperation, invents new religions and curious sects, working up for them strange rituals, or adding to the desiccated forms of current ecclesiasticism extravagant and vulgar devices that are now the sardonic delight of the ungodly.

It does not seem improbable that if once more beauty can be restored to the offices of religion, or rather if the redemptive process now under way can be carried to conclusion, many who are now self-excommunicated from the Church, will thankfully find their way back to the House they have abandoned—less from any fault of their own than from the failure and delinquency of formal religion itself, as this has been made only too visible to the naked eye.

So far as this paper is concerned, the question is this: if the way of beauty is one of the open roads to religion, how is this to be made commonly available? In a word, what is the part to be played by beauty (in the form of all the arts) in modern religious worship, and how, under present circumstances, is this to be made operative?

I do not conceive that it is any part of my business to deal with doctrinal questions (though I might like to do so); but I can at least call attention to the fact that the same test of beauty may be applied to them; that there are (or were) certain dogmatic elements in the later Christian religion, as this is (or once was) interpreted, that are as ugly as any other bad art, and so have acted as stumbling blocks to the traveler in search of faith.

Directly opposed to these "ugly" tenets are those that are "beautiful" in themselves. The whole Catholic Faith is shot through and through with this vital and essential quality of beauty. It is this beauty implicit in the Christian Revelation and its operative system that once was explicit in the material and visible churches and their art.

The Orthodox Russian says that on going into a church one enters Heaven. Like every other Christian for fifteen hundred years, he has used every power he had to make his churches symbols and similes of the Heavenly Jerusalem. From the Church of the Holy Wisdom in Constantinople to the humblest sanctuary in a Russian village, beauty, as the Russian saw beauty, was lavished without stint. In this casket of jewels he found the noblest and most splendid ceremonial and breathed into it the breath of life through the most holy music that the Church has ever known. Largely because of this, and in spite of many other defects and corruptions, he held faithfully to his religion, until at last, in our own day, it was denied him by the "Lord of the World." He holds to it still in exile. The little church of the Seminary of St. Sergius in Paris is a living exposition of the Holy Church of Eastern Orthodoxy, driven back once more into catacombs like those that once sheltered the infant Church in the West.

In a very real sense a great part of the Church is now under a second Neronic persecution and partly isolated and impoverished by indifference. The result of this is easily to be seen in the secular world at large. Until religion once more is accepted as the guiding light of human life, the world must continue wandering in fatal darkness. Is not one road to salvation to be found in the restoration of beauty to the material showing forth of the Faith, in making of churches the symbolical forecast of Heaven, and worship vital through the ministry of beauty?

To this end there must be a new outpouring of artistic power, instigated by a new consciousness of its sanctity and dynamic force. Once more every church must become a focus of beauty. The tendency to reduce a church to the level of "the world without"; to secularize it into the semblance of a theatre or a lecture hall, to banish shrines and statues and pictures (or sterilize them by the "modern touch"); to attempt a fictitious popularity by way of secular activities and startling and frequently uncouth novelties learned from the promoter, the efficiency expert and the advertising agency:—all this is but the sign of decadence: the selling of the birthright for a mess of pottage which, in the end, proves to be without any nutritive value.

The task has been well begun during the last few years; but it is uphill work. One must contend against the strongest imaginable combination of prejudices and superstitions. These are of two sorts. There is, first, the heritage of ignorance and fear from the dark ages of the sixteenth century—I am speaking now more particularly of non-Catholic Christianity: ignorance of authentic history, instigated by protagonists of propaganda; fear of beauty because all that we now have in Christian art was engendered and formulated by and through Catholicism; fear that the acceptance of beauty means that awful thing—"surrender to superstition." Second, there is the equally mistaken idea, already referred to, that religion may be made popular if it is patently affiliated to what we call modern civilization—its formularies, its methods and its outward showing, through building and other arts, made closely to follow the principles and the tendencies of the times.

Some of the positions assumed under the first heading are very curious. There are clergy and congregations which, at a pinch, will accept two candles on an altar (particularly if they are not lighted), but not six under any circumstances; crosses so long as they are void of the symbol of Redemption; figures of saints if they are not given that title; a linen chasuble but not colored vestments. Much is readily accepted in liturgics and ceremonial so long as it has little significance, no implications of real meaning—just as, for example, some Protestant churches will permit no altar candles, but will arrange for every member of a congregation to carry a lighted taper at a "Feast of Lights."

As Chesterton said: "There is no arguing with the choice of the soul." So in this case there is really nothing to be done for those people except to wait and hope for the coming of further enlightenment and a salutary banishment of fear. It is fear, after all, that lies at the root of the matter, as it does in so many other fields of mental activity. If ever the world needed courage it is at this juncture. The recovery of courage might well begin in religion and in its ways of outward expression.

The case is very different when it comes to the

matter of the secularization of religion, what may be called the "domestication" of the church fabric and its approximation to the customary environment of "the man in the street." This attitude, which is found almost wholly in Evangelical Protestant circles, is based on a total misconception of the nature of a church building and what it ought to be like. Instead of "homelike", it ought to be deliberately "otherworldly"; that is to say, it ought in every possible way to differentiate itself from everything one is familiar with in the home, the place of business, the office and the street. A church, as the Russians say, should be, insofar as man can make it so, a symbol and a forecast of Heaven. "The world is too much with us, late and soon; getting and spending, we lay waste our powers." This is particularly true in this day and generation. The Church and its Sacraments, the church building and its manifold beauties of ornament and ceremonial, exist for the one great purpose of restoring and replenishing spiritual powers that are laid waste in the processes of our current life. The moment one passes the portal of a church, whether it be a cathedral or the house of worship of a little country parish, he should find himself in a *milieu* cut off, by closing doors, from "the world without."

I know of two churches, one Roman Catholic, the other Presbyterian, that have supremely significant names. The first is called "The Gate of Heaven"; the other "The House of Hope". Each dedication is a definition in itself. A church is indeed the gate of Heaven and is also the house of hope. Beauty, like faith, is in a real sense "the substance of things hoped for; the evidence of things not seen". Unless a church can be instinct with this, it is not a church, and cannot discharge its function.

Beauty is, then, one of the chief ways of approach by the masses of men and women to religion. That beauty is canalized in and through the material fabric, the liturgies, the ceremonies, all the arts. If, instead of building quite so many Sunday Schools, parish houses and community centers (useful as all these may be), the Church would enter upon a consistent campaign for the restoration of beauty to those places where beauty preëminently belongs, great spiritual miracles would follow. I know that this is so. I have seen it happen in specific instances, in the case of parish churches, and school and college chapels, where an early ugliness has been superseded by such a degree of beauty as it has been possible to create in them in these latter and indifferent days. Under the impact of new and dynamic beauty, congregations have increased, sometimes doubled, while time after time "those that came to scoff remained to pray."

Beauty is man's inalienable heritage. It is one of his natural rights, on a par with his right to life, liberty and the pursuit of happiness. Modern civilization has denied to man this right, filched it from him, giving him instead much ugliness of thought and act and environment. This birthright cannot be restored to him except by concrete and operative religion, for this alone can act as a corrective of the wrong ideas and the worse results of a way of life that won away from beauty's spiritual dynamic. Religion, by cosmic necessity, brought art, which is the precipitation of beauty, into being. After four thousand years it became negligent of its trust. Now the Church has begun to recognize again its duty. If the Church will, it can open the road so long closed, and by this road, not as the only path, but as one of the chief highways, an alienated world may return to its age-old loyalty; and man will know once more the better way of life.